BRANCH LINE TO SELSEY

Vic Mitchell and Keith Smith

Other albums featuring Chichester

Branch Lines to Midhurst

Branch Lines around Midhurst

Chichester to Portsmouth

West Sussex Railways in the 1980s

Other Colonel Stephens albums

Branch Line to Tenterden

Branch Line to Hawkhurst

Branch Line to Shrewsbury

East Kent Light Railway

Steaming through West Sussex

This includes a rare picture of Colonel Stephens Ford lorry coupled to a railbus at Selsey

For the complete current list of Middleton Press railway albums and Sussex books, write or telephone -

 **Middleton Press**

Easebourne Lane, Midhurst, West Sussex.. GU29 9AZ
Tel: 0730 813169

First published 1983
Reprinted May 1991

ISBN 0 906520 04 5

© Middleton Press 1991

Published by Middleton Press
Easebourne Lane
Midhurst
West Sussex
Tel: (0730) 813169

Printed & bound by Biddles Ltd,
Guildford and Kings Lynn

INDEX

AUTHOR'S NOTES

As the tramway was converted to a railway by the stroke of a pen in 1924, the two terms were used indiscriminately by the proprietors to describe their line. We have therefore taken the same liberty. Similarly, the words train and tram must be considered to be synonymous.

To justify the title, we contend that whilst the line was not a branch of a main line company, it certainly was a branch shown on the map of the national railway network.

The maps used herein are all to the scale of 25" to 1 mile, unless otherwise shown. The undated timetables and advertisements are reproduced from a booklet published by the Hundred of Manhood and Selsey Tramways Co. Ltd. in 1912.

Strangers to the Selsey peninsula may like to know that the popular pronunciation of the place names is as follows-
CHIchester – as in CHI ck.
SIDlesham – as in SIDney.
SELSEY – thus-sells-ee.

ACKNOWLEDGEMENTS

In addition to those named under the photographs who have so willingly supplied copies of their own work or loaned prints from their collections, we would like thank the following for their help: C. Attwell, N. Fosberry, R. Good, M.J. Grainger, R. Harmer, A. Hill, A.A. Ogden, J. Miller, J. Prior, P. Shaw, N. Stanyon and our ever tolerant wives who assist us in so many ways. To those photographers whose unmarked prints we have used without giving credit, we apologise in advance.

We are grateful to C.R. Gordon Stuart for the opportunity of reproducing tickets from his collection.

GEOGRAPHICAL SETTING

The coastal plain is at its widest in the vicinity of Chichester, extending southwards to form the Selsey peninsula. Until the early nineteenth century Selsey was situated on an island and in 1807 a "wadeway" was constructed to link it to the mainland. In former years the island was noted for its seal population which gave rise to the name of Seal's Ea. Marine deposits, particularly on the western shore, gradually united the island to the mainland. This process was aided by small schemes culminating in the complete reclamation of Pagham Harbour from the sea in 1876. Vast acreages of pasture were thus created until the sea wall was dramatically breached a few days before Christmas 1910, leaving the geography much as it is today.

The other feature of note was the Chichester City Canal which entered tidal waters at Birdham lock.

Before the construction of a road to Selsey, a ferry linked the island to the mainland. The group of houses at the south end of the causeway are still known as Ferry.

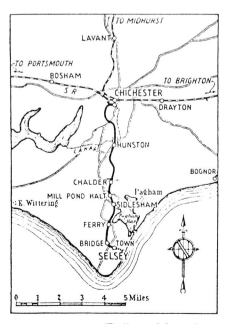

(Railway Magazine).

The one inch to the mile OS map of 1920 shows the LBSCR main line running east-west to the south of Chichester with the Hundred of Manhood and Selsey Tramway (HMST) shown thus – ┼┼┼

There are several errors – the line was never called the Chichester & Selsey Tramy.; Hoe Farm and Golf Links Halts were private (the company stated that tickets would only be issued to persons entitled to use these stations); Selsey Bridge Halt is omitted; Selsey Town station is shown as a halt!; Selsey Beach is shown as the terminus when the rails had been taken up nearly 20 years earlier.

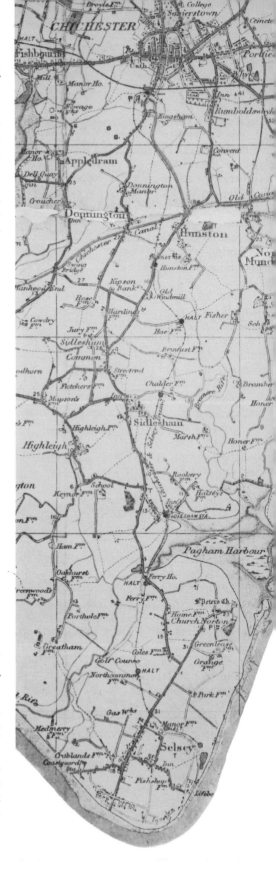

HISTORICAL BACKGROUND

The LBSCR from Brighton reached Chichester in 1846 and was soon extended to Portsmouth. In 1896 the Light Railways Act was passed which enabled local lines to be constructed cheaply by allowing lower track and safety standards, but subject to severe speed restrictions. About this time a group of influential local people met together to consider building a railway to Selsey, and found that they did not even need to obtain a Light Railway Order for the compulsory purchase of land as it was all available by negotiation (or the old-boy network) some being obtained at a mere £10 per acre, cheap even in those days. The coming of rail transport increased land values, so that landowners were willing to cooperate, especially with the offer of a railway siding close to their farms. The line was therefore built under the little used Railway Construction Facilities Act of 1864. The enterprising proprietors decided to form a tramway company so that they would be free of the extensive legislation under which railway companies were forced to operate. Moreover tramways could operate in (or across) public highways without special arrangements, so the company was not obliged to provide normal safety measures at their numerous level crossings. Thus the line operated for many years without legal authority, not even coming under the scrutiny of the Railway Inspectorate of the Board of Trade.

Traffic commenced on 27th August 1897, stopping short of Selsey Town station, the building of which was not finished in time for the opening. The line was extended a further ½ mile to the Beach in the following year. Construction cost and land purchase amounted to £21,570 whilst £3,268 was initially spent on rolling stock. Receipts soon reached a very satisfactory level and the Edwardian period was one of great prosperity for this much needed railway – sorry, tramway. With new coaches, a new locomotive, adequate track and a profusion of passengers, there were no indications of the laughing stock that the line was to become in its declining years.

Catastrophe struck the company on the night of 10th December, 1910 when the sea, with a mighty roar, broke through the bank on the east side of the peninsula flooding 2000 acres within one hour and immersing the railway in water up to 12 ft. deep. Incidentally, Selsey gasworks was also flooded, cracking the retorts and thus depriving the villagers of gaslight and gas for cooking their Christmas dinners. Fortunately, the railway was in its prime and prosperous enough to pay for a mile-long embankment up to 15ft high, to be built to carry its line across what had become Pagham Harbour again.

In 1913, the directors decided to seek powers under a Light Railway Order to build a branch from Hunston to West Itchenor and East Wittering. At West Itchenor a 200 ft. long pier was proposed to receive vessels of up to 800 tons. World War I intervened and the scheme was abandoned

The decline in passenger traffic was brought about by the increase in private motoring and the commencement of a rival bus service which was more convenient than "the tram", since it operated into the centre of Chichester and throughout the length of the straggling village of Selsey.

In 1924, the directors decided to form a railway company to take over the tramway company. The reason for this is not clear. Our suggestion is that, in view of their declining fortunes, they might wish to seek a take-over bid and that the only likely source of this was the newly created Southern Railway which was presumably constituted to incorporate legally operated railways, and not dubious tramways of convenience. The grandiose title chosen was the "West Sussex Railway – Selsey Tramway Section", with expansion no doubt still in mind.

A steady decline in passenger figures was arrested in 1927, but only for two years, as the following figures show-

	Passengers	Receipts		
		£	s	d
1919	102,292	3,912.13.		0
1920	79,574	3,272. 1.		9
1921	66,349	2,406.14.		0
1922	60,203	1,910.16.		8
1923	44,977	1,404. 6.		4
1924	31,352	949. 8.		2
1925	21,762	799. 6.		1
1926	17,171	685. 4.		2
1927	22,475	514.15.		11
1928	35,493	749.16.		8
1929	22,676	556.11.		5
1930	15,904	354. 4.		11
1931	13,416	279.15.		2
1932	20,967	427.17.		9
1933	21,088	427. 9.		11

In 1933 the single fare was a mere 8d but this failed to attract passengers who would prefer to pay 11d to Southdown Motor Services for the comfort and reliability offered. It was a wholly uneconomic fare, as can be seen by the fact that the Southern Railway would have charged 11½d for a journey of the same length. Freight traffic, however, was fairly steady, yielding an income of around £2000 in each of the post war years.

INCOME 1933 – TRAFFIC

Description	Tons	Local £ s d	Through £ s d	TOTAL £ s d
Passengers		381. 2. 3	46. 7. 8	427. 9.11
Season tickets		6.17.10	–	6.17.10
Goods	4464	78.11. 4	638. 1. 3	716.12. 7
Minerals	2260	–	166.17. 9	166.17. 9
Coal and Coke	5224	–	692. 3. 6	692. 3. 6
Parcels		16. 4. 0	241. 1. 9	257. 5. 9
Miscellaneous traffic		11. 1. 9	45. 9. 9	56.11. 6
Live stock		–	15. 2	15. 2
Mails and Parcel Post				41. 7. 9
Miscellaneous Receipts				3.17. 1
		493.17. 2	1830.16.10	2369.18.10

INCOME 1933 – RENT

		£	s.	d.
Chichester	Anglo-American	8.	8.	0.
	Shell-Mex	94.	0.	0.
	Sadler (siding and land)	12.	12.	0.
	Bottrell (Coal wharf)	4.	4.	0.
Chalder	Charlton (Coal wharf)	5.	0.	0.
Selsey	Ansell & Son (coal)	10.	0.	0.
	H. Prior	7.	0.	0.
	Trojan Brick Co. (Siding and land)	3.	0.	0.
	Four cottages	132.	0.	0.
	1 garden			9.
		279.	4.	9.

WEEKLY EXPENDITURE – 1933

	£	s.	d.
Traffic			
Superintendent	3.	1.	6.
Selsey – Part time temporary Clerk	1.	1.	0.
Hunston-Sidlesham. Lad Porter (also performs Parcels Delivery)		13.	0.
Chichester – Station Agent	2.	10.	0.
Guard-Conductor	1.	0.	0.
Locomotive Running			
Fitter Driver	3.	3.	0.
Fireman Labourer	2.	0.	0.
Rail-car Driver	2.	12.	1.
Engineer's			
Ganger	2.	3.	6.
Undermen (3)	1.	13.	0.
	1.	10.	0.
	1.	10.	0.
Total	22.	17.	1.

The wages were for a nominal 54-hour week which included working until 9 pm on Saturdays and 11 pm on Wednesdays! How times have changed.

Whilst direct operating expenses amounted to nearly £1,200 per annum there was a massive debt of £5,274 in debenture interest and £7,467 owing to the executors of Col. Stephens.

These figures speak for themselves; they also told the directors that the end was nigh and they also failed to interest the Southern Railway in making an offer for the undertaking. Services therefore ceased on 19th January, 1935, there having been only one train a day during the previous eight weeks. Earlier, the Southern Railway examined the possibility of taking it over as a "going" concern but decided against it.

Little remains to be seen today – fragments of platform edge at Hunston and Chalder; a chalk embankment in Pagham Harbour and a canal bridge abutment. A living memorial exists in a modern public house called the "Selsey Tram" not far from the old route, south of Chichester.

ACCIDENTS

There is no record of collisions between trains, no doubt due to the fact that normally there was only one running. The driver was obliged to carry the "train staff" for the two sections of line and at busy times it was possible to despatch two trains in the same direction by the use of a "ticket".

The only fatal accident recorded was due to defective permanant way and is illustrated herein by photograph numbers 60 and 61. The same fault gave rise to numerous derailments.

Level crossing of roads caused a large number of accidents and larger numbers of near-misses which are now local folk-lore. As late as 1932, a Ministry of Transport inspector making enquiries about a collision at Stockbridge Road asked why the line had never been inspected. He was apparently satisfied with the explanation the line was a tramway and not a railway! After this, all trains were ordered to stop at crossings so that a crew member could see them safely across the road.

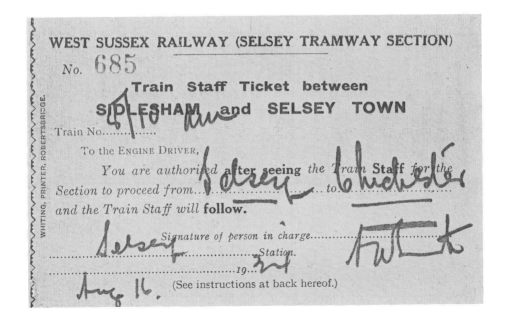

THE ENGINEER

The first directors of the line appointed Mr. H.F. Stephens, still in his twenties, as their engineer to supervise construction and to procure the necessary equipment. Holman Fred Stephens was trained in civil and mechanical engineering and quickly built a reputation as a dynamic and competent light railway engineer. It was his novel and unique methods of equipping and operating railways that made him a legend in his lifetime and gave the branch line to Selsey its quaint character. He became Lt. Col. Stephens in 1914, after which he was simply known on the line as "the Colonel". He soon became a director and eventually the majority shareholder.

His engineering reputation made him much sought after by the directors of minor railways. He eventually controlled a dozen or so lines which included the following – (approximate mileages in brackets) Kent & East Sussex (21), East Kent (14), Weston Clevedon & Portishead (14), Shropshire &

Montgomeryshire (27) and other short lines with equally lengthy impressive titles. He controlled his empire of fragile railways from an office sandwiched between shops in Salford Terrace, Tonbridge. On 1st April, 1923, the Colonel was appointed civil engineer and locomotive superintendent to the ailing Festiniog Railway and its weakly infant offspring, the Welsh Highland Railway. In his history of the former J.I.C. Boyd says – "even in those days, the king of minor railways, Col. Stephens had achieved a particular notoriety and fame because of the number of buccolic and decrepit undertakings with which he was connected. At a single move the engineering side of the Festiniog activities was moved to Kent". K. & S. Turner in their history of the Shropshire & Montgomeryshire Light Railway eloquently summarise as follows–

"in the history of the railways of these islands, Colonel Stephens stands out as one of the most extraordinary personages ever; his name is virtually – and justly – synonymous with the British Light Railway and for that involvement, together with his idiosyncratic methods of operation, his memory is deservedly venerated by all lovers of such lines. To all intents and purposes, Stephens collected railways in the way that another might open grocery shops".

He died a bachelor in 1931 before his empire began to fall.

LOCOMOTIVES

Nos.	Name	Wheels	Builder	No.	Built	Acquired	Scrap	Notes
2	SELSEY	2-4-2 T	Peckett	681	1897	1897	1935	1
3 or 2	SIDLESHAM	0-6-0 ST	Manning Wardle	21	1861	1907	c1932	2
4 or 2	HESPERUS	0-4-2 ST	Neilson	1661	1872	1912	1931	3
5 or 2	RINGING ROCK	0-6-0 ST	Manning Wardle	890	1883	1917	1935	4
1 or 3	CHICHESTER	0-4-2 T	Longbottoms	–	1847	1897	1913	5
6 or 4	CHICHESTER	0-6-0 ST	Hudswell Clarke	635	1903	1919	1932	6
7 or 4	MOROUS	0-6-0 ST	Manning Wardle	178	1866	1924	1936	7

Notes

1. The only loco to arrive new on the line.
2. Four previous owners. Rebuilt by Hawthorn Leslie.
3. From Plymouth Devonport & S.W. Junc. Ply. Originally 3'6" gauge.
4. Fourth-hand. Was No. 5 until 1935.
5. Built as an 0-6-0 ST and rebuilt by Avonsides and Pecketts.
6. New to Naylor Bros., Huddersfield.
7. Stratford & Midland Rly No. 1 until 1910 when bought by the Colonel for his S & M line.

PASSENGER VEHICLES

Nos.	Wheels	Type	Source
1	8	Saloon	New from Falcons in 1897
2	8	Saloon	New from Falcons in 1897
3	8	Saloon/Brake	New from Falcons in 1897
4	8	Saloon	New from Hurst Nelson c 1900
5	4	Saloon	ex-Lambourn Valley 1910
6	4	Saloon	ex-Lambourn Valley 1910
7	4	Saloon	ex-Lambourn Valley 1910
–	4	5 compartments	ex-LCDR c 1916
–	4	5 compartments	ex-LCDR c 1916
–	4	2 compartments/brake	ex-LCDR c 1916
–	4	5 compartments	ex-LCDR c 1916
–	6	5 compartments	ex-LCDR 1931 (SR 1636)
–	6	4 compartments/brake	ex-LCDR 1931 (SR 3639)
–	4	Petrol railcar	Wolseley – Siddeley c 1921
–	4	Petrol railcar	Shefflex 1928
–	4	Petrol railcar	Shefflex 1928
–	4	Petrol railcar	Edmunds (Ford engines) 1923
–	4	Petrol railcar	Edmunds (Ford engines) 1923

CHICHESTER

1.   The crowds are seen here gathering around the terminus (and on the gasworks roof!) to witness the departure of the first train on 27th August 1897. Inexplicably it was an hour late arriving from Selsey – a bad start for a line that was to become well known in its later years for unpunctuality. When the locomotive "Chichester" with three new bogie coaches eventually arrived, it became apparent that the platform was so short that only the engine and two coaches could be accommodated; more-over the train had to be propelled out of the station before the engine could be run over the crossover and onto the other end of the train. The coaches then had to be pushed back into the platform. This inconvenient method of working was eventually overcome by lengthening the platform. Notice the appalling alignment of the rails in the crossover and the lack of locomotive water supply.
(R. Mitchell Coll.)

2. "Selsey" was the only locomotive supplied new to the line and is seen here in Edwardian days in smart condition with only its front coupling missing. It was also the only 2-4-2 ever used on the line. (L.E. Hall/R.C. Riley Coll.)

3. Beyond the coach can be seen two early vending machines (then called slot machines); behind them, the main line station building, and beyond it, the cathedral spire. Notice also the curtains at the windows of the saloon compartment and the end verandah. (R. Mitchell Coll.)

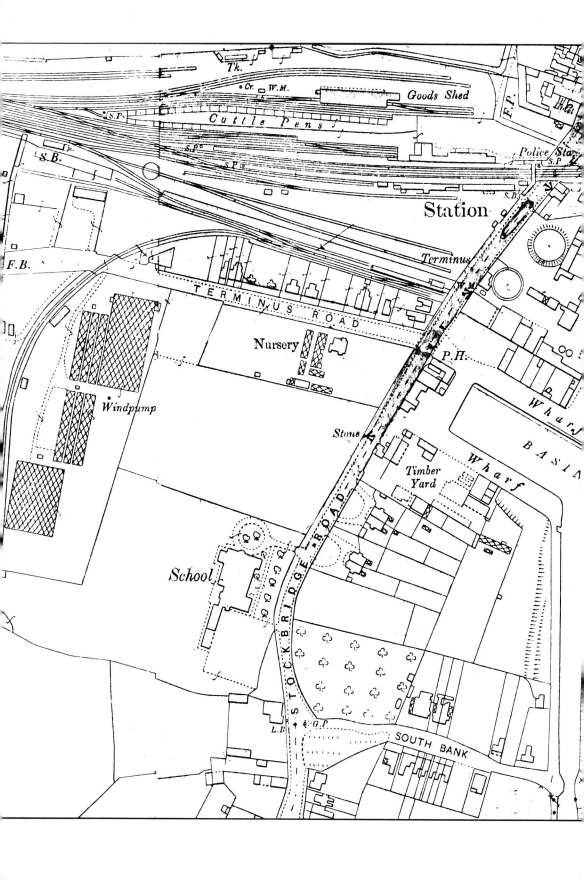

Tk.

Cr. W.M.

Goods Shed

S.P.

Cattle Pens

S.B.

S.P.

S.P.

F.P.

Police Sta.

S.P.

S.B.

Station

F.B.

Terminus

W.M.

TERMINUS ROAD

Nursery

P.H.

Wharf

Windpump

BASIN

Stone

Wharf

Timber
Yard

School

STOCKBRIDGE ROAD

L.B.

G.P.

SOUTH BANK

4. This is the first locomotive on the line to be named "Chichester" and was obviously cherished by its driver who had adorned it with a cross and stars, a practice common on Indian railways. At the end of the lengthy goods train is a single coach for passengers who would have had a rough ride when the loose couplings of the wagons snatched taut as the train started away. The picture is dated 1903. (Col. Stephens Rly. Museum, Tenterden).

This map of 1912 shows the terminus of the Hundred of Manhood & Selsey Tramway and the station of the LBSCR. The line to Selsey curves southward on the left of the map past greenhouses which are shown as chequered areas and are now replaced by factories.

5. Photographed in 1915, "Selsey" is seen here displaying the rerailing jack, essential equipment for all locomotive crews on the line but giving no more comfort to passengers than the now familiar call to fasten safety belts before take off. Behind the fence are the sidings of the LBSCR. (K. Nunn/R.C. Riley Coll.)

TABLE OF FARES

Saloon Fares are 3d. above Ordinary Fares as below for single journey.

FROM	To Chichester		To Hunston		To Hoe Farm Private Stn.		To Chalder		To Sidlesham		To Ferry		To Golf Links Private Stn.		To Selsey	
	Single	Ret'n	Single	Ret'n	Single	Ret'n	Single	Ret'n	Single	Ret'n	Single	Ret'n	Single	Ret'n	Single	Ret'n
	s. d.	s. d.	s. d.	s. d.	s. d.	s. d.	s. d.	s. d.	s. d.	s. d.	s. d.	s. d.	s. d.	s. d.	s. d.	s. d.
CHICHESTER	—	—	3		4		4		5	10	7		7½	1 3	7½	1 2
HUNSTON	3	—	—	—	1	—	2	—	4	—	6	—	6	—	6	—
HOE FARM (Private Station)	4	—	1	—	—	—	1	—	3	—	4	—	5	—	5	—
CHALDER	4	—	2	—	1	—	—	—	2	—	4	—	5	—	5	—
SIDLESHAM	5	10	4	—	3	—	2	—	—	—	2	—	4	—	4	6
FERRY	7	—	6	—	4	—	4	—	2	—	—	—	2	—	3	—
GOLF LINKS (Private Stat'n)	7½	1 3	6	—	5	—	5	—	4	—	2	—	—	—	2	—
SELSEY	7½	1 3	6	—	5	—	5	—	4	6	3	—	2	—	—	—

Children under 12 years of age Half-Price.   Under 3 years of age free.

Dogs (accompanied by Passenger) ... ... 6d. each Single or Return.
Bicycles & Perambulators (accompanied by Passenger) 6d. ,, ,,
Tricycles & Tandem Bicycles 9d. each Single or Return.
Motor Bicycles, uncharged with gas, oil, or other inflammable liquid or vapour 9d. each Single or Return.

All Return Tickets are available for return within one month including day of issue.
Tickets from and to Hoe Farm and Golf Links Stations will be issued only to persons entitled to use these Stations.

SEASON TICKET RATES.

FROM	TO	SALOON COMPARTMENT.							ORDINARY COMPARTMENT.						
		Ann'l	Six m'nth	Three m'nth	Two m'nth	One m'nth	Two weeks	One week	Ann'l	Six m'nth	Three m'nth	Two m'nth	One m'nth	Two weeks	One week
		s. d.	s. d.	s. d.	s. d.	s. d.	s. d.	s. d.	s. d.	s. d.	s. d.	s. d.	s. d.	s. d.	s. d.
SELSEY	FERRY	80 0	45 0	27 6	20 0	12 0	...	...	55 0	40 0	25 0	18 0	10 0	...	...
,,	SIDLESHAM	100 0	55 0	32 6	25 0	15 0	...	...	85 0	45 0	28 0	22 6	12 6	...	...
,,	CHALDER	120 0	65 0	40 0	30 0	17 6	...	...	110 0	60 0	36 8	27 6	14 0	...	...
,,	HUNSTON	130 0	70 0	42 6	32 6	18 0	...	...	115 0	62 6	37 6	30 0	15 0	...	...
,,	CHICHESTER	150 0	80 0	50 0	37 6	20 0	11 0	6 0	140 0	75 0	46 8	32 6	18 0	9 6	5 0
CHICHESTER	HUNSTON	80 0	45 0	27 6	20 0	12 0	...	...	55 0	40 0	25 0	18 0	10 0	...	...
,,	CHALDER	100 0	55 0	32 6	25 0	15 0	...	...	85 0	45 0	28 0	22 6	12 6	...	...
,,	SIDLESHAM	120 0	65 0	40 0	30 0	17 6	...	...	110 0	60 0	36 8	27 6	14 0	...	...
,,	FERRY SIDING	130 0	70 0	42 6	32 6	18 0	...	...	115 0	62 6	37 6	30 0	15 0	...	...
,,	SELSEY	150 0	80 0	50 0	37 6	20 0	11 0	6 0	140 0	75 0	46 8	32 6	18 0	9 6	5 0

Special Terms for School Children, &c.

6. Water supply for the engines was originally only available at Selsey (from a well) and at Hunston (from a ditch). The latter was inconvenient operationally and unreliable, which forced Col. Stephens to use mains supply at Chichester with the attendant humiliation of paying a water rate. The fireman's posture might have been easy to adopt, but more difficult to recover from, despite the spacious trousers. By 1921, when photographed, the lamp bracket was seldom used for lamps, but it was useful for winding a piece of chain round to hold up the unusual smokebox door. (H.S. Brighty/R.C. Riley Coll.)

The fares table for 1912 is apparently one class only, but for 3d extra one could travel in a saloon! Just as today, Russia must appear to be a classless society, although you can buy hardclass or softclass railway tickets. Similarly the tramway could not appear to be a railway by offering class fares. Another oddity is the limited number of stops at which return tickets were available. Younger readers may need to know that 5p = 1s and 1p = 2.4d.

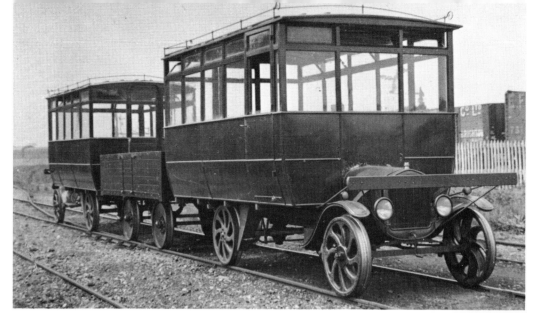

7. In 1923, the first pair of railcars, with luggage trailer, were obtained. The bodies were built by Edmunds of Thetford on Ford Model T chassis. Note the starting handle and sanding gear. Trials had been made about 1921 with a single Wolseley – Siddeley car which was hauled on its return journey by a lorry chassis. (E.C. Griffith Coll.)

The reason for the special offer from Chichester being available on a Thursday was that it was early closing day in the city. Restall appears to be a pioneer of what the airlines today call apex fares. 6d off if you book in advance and you take a chance with weather! Notice the confusion about trams and trains in adjacent advertisements.

Cheap Excursion Tickets,

CHICHESTER

TO

. . SELSEY,

Return 9d. Fare.

Will be issued by the 2.15 p.m tram

EVERY SUNDAY,

and by the 2.20 p.m. tram

EVERY THURSDAY,

Available to return by any tram on day of issue only.

Restall's Excursions

EVERY THURSDAY

During July, August & September,
except August 1st.

─ RESTALL'S CHEAP TRAINS ─

RUN FROM

London Bridge	...	11.50 a.m.
New Cross ...	...	11.55 a.m,
Victoria ...	...	11.50 a.m.
Clapham Junction...		11.55 a.m.
Balham ...	...	12.0 noon
West Croydon	...	12.15 p.m.

TO

SELSEY-ON-SEA.

Return Fare 3s. if taken before the day

Return Fare 3s. 6d. if taken on the day.

Return Train Leaves Selsey 7.5 p.m.

See Restall's Bills for Conditions, &c.

8. The second pair of petrol railcars to be used were built by the Shefflex Motor Co. of Tinsley, near Sheffield, in 1928. The 1872 Tramways Act required trams to be fitted with mechanical bells. However, it is recorded that "audible means of approach" on these rail buses was provided by an exhaust operated whistle, but this vehicle appears to be fitted with an electric gong. In fact, the roar of the engine could be heard miles off in any case. (J.W. Sparrowe/R.C. Riley Coll.)

9. Adequate water supplies were equally necessary for this form of combustion, although for cooling not heating. The Colonel was also an advocate of good publicity and erected a large sign on the roof of his terminus to attract passengers alighting from main line trains. Unfortunately when this photograph was taken it had decayed and merely read – "S SEY MWAY". (Lens of Sutton).

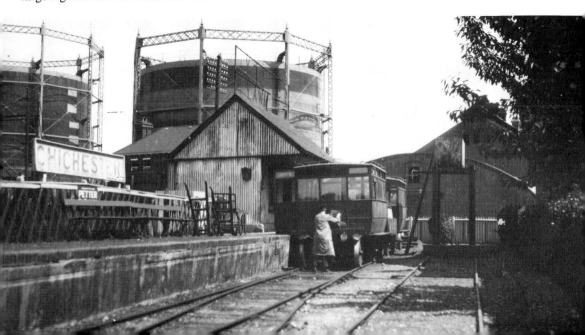

10. "Sidlesham" is seen here on freight transfer duties with a main line goods train in the background. Loco crews were often ridiculed at this location by their counterparts on "Big Brother" about their antiquated neglected engines (M.D. England/NRM).

PARCELS RATES.

The Rates for conveyance of parcels between any pair of Stations on the Selsey Tramways are as follows :

Under 14lbs.	Under 28lbs.	Under 56lbs.	Under 112lbs.
2d. each	**4d. each.**	**6d. each.**	**8d. each.**

Rates are exclusive of collection or delivery.

Senders are requested to insert under the address of parcels sent to Selsey, either " Wait till called for " or " To be delivered." In the absence of any instructions the parcels will be sent out for delivery in the usual way.

Rates for Collection or Delivery at Selsey.

Within the ordinary limits.

Parcels up to 28lbs........	2d. each
,, from 28lbs. to 56lbs.	3d. ,,
,, ,, 56lbs. to 112lbs.	4d. ,,
,, ,, 112lbs. to 224lbs.........	6d. ,,
Consignments from 2 cwts. to 1 ton (inclusive)	3/- per ton.
Truck loads ,, 1 ton to 2 tons ,, ...	2/6 ,,
,, ,, 2 tons to 4 tons ,, ...	2/3 ,
, ,, above 4 tons	2/- ,,

Minimum charge above 1 cwt., 6d.

11. "Sidlesham" simmers between journeys. A pit was dug between the rails at this point so that faults that had developed in the inside motion of the locomotives during the previous eight miles could be dealt with before returning to the other pit by Selsey loco shed. The man on the carriage roof is likely to be have been putting oil into the lights. The houses on the right are the only features remaining today. (Lens of Sutton/R.C. Riley Coll.)

12. The intending traveller's view of a mixed train waiting to leave, on Guy Fawkes day 1928. The residents of Terminus Road were very familiar with mobile bonfires as tramway engines shunted about at the end of their clothes lines on cheap coal with poor draughting. The dip in the platform edge was where the platform extension began. (H.C. Casserley).

13. "Ringing Rock" drifts gently into the terminus from Selsey past the washing with a very mixed train – four open wagons, a van and a secondhand compartment coach in case there were any passengers. (Dr. I.C. Allen)

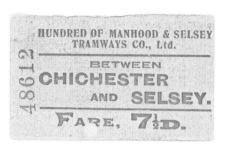

HUNDRED OF MANHOOD & SELSEY
TRAMWAYS CO., Ltd.

BETWEEN
CHICHESTER
AND SELSEY.

FARE, 7½D.

48612

15. What appears to be a peaceful pose of "Ringing Rock" for the photographer is in fact a picture of human misery. Look for the four feet of the footplate crew. On returning from the exertion of shunting five wagons, the engine has suffered a major internal disorder preventing it even reaching the pit at the platform. The unfortunate men are having to dismantle it on the spot with washing, in either sense, far from their minds. This engine is recorded as having run for three weeks on only one cylinder whilst a new cylinder cover was being made, not one of the remaining locos being serviceable at the time. (Dr. I.C. Allen)

14. Having shunted the coach off, the wagons are propelled back into the exchange siding, the white gate post marking the boundary between the two companies. Whilst the engine discharges steam from places it should not, the driver looks out to see if the washing has yet been taken off the line. (Dr. I.C. Allen)

16. The end of the line – in both senses. After closure in January 1935, "Ringing Rock" and the chassis of the Shefflex railcars await the scrap merchant. (H.C. Casserley).

17. "Ringing Rock" was last in steam on 24th January 1935 after which it was deliberately struck a mortal blow – a wedge was hammered into the boiler to prevent any further use. The former loyal servants of the company are shown here axle-deep in weeds, four years after the Colonel had himself been laid to rest. (Lens of Sutton).

18. The view from Stockbridge Road, the main road south from the city. The timber framed, corrugated iron clad buildings were standard throughout the line and were also used on the other railways of Colonel Stephens. (J.W. Sparrowe/R.C. Riley Coll.)

19. The terminal area was acquired by the Southern Railway, who removed the fence, platform and building, laying in new sidings as part of their extended coal yard, seen here in 1952. (H.C. Casserley).

20. The driver's face, as if in a cameo, is illuminated fully by the afternoon sun as "Selsey" chugs over Terminus Road in 1911. (H.L. Hopwood/K. Nunn Coll./LCGB).

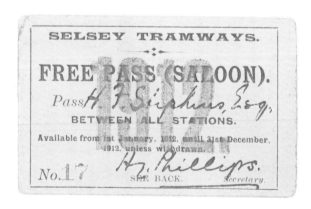

SELSEY TRAMWAYS.

FREE PASS (SALOON).

Pass *H. F. Stephens, Esq,*

BETWEEN ALL STATIONS.

Available from 1st January, 1912, until 31st December, 1912, unless withdrawn.

No. 17   SEE BACK.   *Hy. Phillips.* Secretary.

21. Busy factories now stand where peaceful glasshouses once were, south of Terminus Road. One of the original saloon coaches was sufficient for traffic in April 1911. (H.L. Hopwood/K. Nunn Coll./LCGB).

22. "Selsey" returning from Selsey on 12th June 1915, travelling over the sharpest curve on the line (6 chains radius) on which a 6 mph speed limit was imposed. (K. Nunn Coll./ LCGB).

23. A snap taken from the moving train, as it approaches Stockbridge Road in September 1933, on its journey south. Cattle grids reduced the risk of animals wandering on to the line. (T. Middlemass).

24. The distinctive Manning Wardle cab shape is seen well as "Sidlesham" climbs away from the Stockbridge Road level crossing and a main line train steams away in the distance. The safety valves were altered at a later date. (E.C. Griffith Coll.)

25. An early view at the same location showing "Selsey" with three of the four coaches bought new by the company. The last vehicle was built by Hurst Nelson, the others by Falcon of Loughborough. (R. Mitchell Coll.)

26. With the houses of Stockbridge Road in the background No. 2 ambles along with the 4.20 to Selsey on 12th June 1915 near to the point where the line began to run parallel to the Chichester canal. (K. Nunn Coll./LCGB).

THEIR FIRST SWIMMING LESSON

SWANS NEST WITHIN A FEW FEET OF CHICHESTER & SELSEY TRAM

27. A popular postcard view emphasising the rural charm of the tramway in the vicinity of the canal. The winch was operated by a windlass which was removable to prevent unauthorised use. The abutments can still be seen by canal side walkers, (WSCC Library Service).

29. Part of this fine view of the lifting bridge and "Sidlesham" graced the cover of the last edition of E.C. Griffiths' informative book on the line. The full picture reveals that it was necessary to remove fish plates before raising the bridge. Additional lifting tackle had been provided since the previous picture was taken. (Lens of Sutton).

←——

28. It appears that five men were required to raise the canal bridge. In the early nineteenth century, this waterway formed part of "London's Lost Route to the Sea", ably described by P.A.L. Vine in his book of that title. In the early years of the tramway, small sea-going vessels of the type seen here were horse drawn from Birdham lock to Chichester basin. The bridge was owned by Chichester City Council who charged £2 per annum for the passage of trains over it. (Chichester District Museum).

HUNSTON

30. Looking up the 1 in 117 gradient towards Chichester soon after the opening of the line. The reverse curves which caused problems for steam-shy engines attempting to start trains up the incline, can be clearly seen. They were eliminated by straightening the track in 1908. Down trains stopping to take water completely blocked the level crossing. This inconvenience to local road users was mitigated by relocating the water tank at the other end of the platform. (Lens of Sutton).

31. Hunston was the only intermediate station to be staffed. Duties involved handling parcels, hand pumping water for the locomotives from the ditch into the tank and supervising goods traffic at the single siding. The company, always out for a bargain, appointed Mr. Gilbert, a man with only one arm for these "light" duties. By 1933, the staff consisted of a "lad porter" at 13 shillings a week and he was expected to deliver the parcels around the village. The average number of passengers joining trains here at this time was 10½ per day. (R. Mitchell Coll.)

HUNDRED OF MAN

Kiln

Brick Works

F.B.

H

U

N

Station

Tank

L.B

The 1912 edition reveals a loop provided for the brickworks and a siding at the station, but neither are shown on the 1932 plans. The former trackbed northwards from the level crossing to the canal is now a public footpath.

32. Mr. W. Bishop tells of a journey to remember, of which his picture illustrates a part.

When a boy I remember my father telling me about journeys he and my mother used to make on the Hundred of Manhood and Selsey Tramways as it was known in the early 1900s. He spoke about the tramway type coaches with transverse seats and covered platforms and steps at each end. It was quite an adventure to travel after dark as the coaches were only lit by oil lamps, making it impossible to read a book or paper. My father never did tell me why he and my mother made these trips on the tramway but as it was during their courting days I did not ask questions.

Thirty years later, during October 1933, I was employed at Fratton loco running shed and having a holiday I decided I would like to visit the tramway which had been re named the West Sussex Railway. My future wife and I travelled from Fratton station to Chichester by push and pull train, made up of two ex-LB SCR coaches and a Stroudley DI class loco. Arriving at Chichester station, we made our way to the tramway station a few yards down the road. Here the train was already waiting at the single platform station. I think the loco was "Morous", as "Ringing Rock" was out of steam in a dead end siding. Judging by the weeds around it, it looked as though it had been there quite some time. I enquired of the conductor-cum-guard as to when the train would be leaving. He did not know, as the regular loco was out of service and the one they had was short of steam owing to leaking tubes in the fire-box. There were no other passengers and later the guard said they were ready to leave. Upon asking for two return tickets to Selsey he said he would collect our fares on arrival, as we would probably want to return by bus. Not a chance, as the only reason we were travelling on the train was to see how much it had improved since my parents young days. We took our seats in the first coach, one of two ex-London, Chatham and Dover Railway six-wheelers. Thus began a most interesting journey back into the past. After leaving the station and crossing the road, we continued over the canal bridge where the train came to an abrupt halt. Being in open country I looked out of the carriage window. I saw the loco travelling up the line on its own and photographed it. The guard being on the track I enquired what was wrong. He said, "Owing to the leaking fire box the tanks were empty and the loco was going to the next station for water." Fortunately this was Hunston, the only station between Chichester and Selsey where it was possible to get water. When the loco returned we once again proceeded on our way. Before we could run into Hunston Station the driver had to stop at the level crossing for the fireman to proceed to the middle of the road to stop all road traffic. This occurred at three or four level crossings on the way, and was not good for time keeping. After leaving Hunston we were again brought to a halt in open country. This time it was for the guard and fireman to round up a horse which had strayed onto the track. There were no other incidents and we arived at Selsey after taking well over one hour for the journey. We were still the only passengers on the train, and when I asked the guard for return tickets he could hardly believe it.

In those days Selsey was not a holiday resort as it is today, and after leaving the station we made our way to the sea front. Here we found much of the beach privately owned, and the people we spoke to made it clear to us that they did not want visitors, especially those who came by the 'Selsey Bumper.' We returned to the station where we found the loco in the shed, having given up after our journey. There being no one about I was able to look around the station and yard freely. As there was no one available, we could not get any information as to whether the railway had closed for the day. It looked as though we would be returning by bus after all. Before we could make a decision I was surprised to see a bus coming towards the station on the rails. When it stopped at the platform I saw that there were two four-wheeled Ford motor buses, fitted with rail wheels and coupled together back to back, with a small four wheel wagon between them. As with the train there were no passengers, only the driver and conductor-guard. We were informed if we wanted to go to Chichester we would have to travel in one of the buses as they were running in place of the train. The timetable seemed to have been scrapped and we left when the crew were ready. We took our seats with them in the leading bus, which was towing the wagon and trailing bus. It was not long before we regretted this decision as the fumes and noise from the engine were terrific. I think it must have been running on paraffin oil. Owing to the uneven track and bad joints one had to hold on to the seats, and conversation was impossible. It would have been much more comfortable and quicker to have returned by Southdown bus, but we could travel on those any day, where as the journey we were making was to be only once in my life time, as the railway closed before I could visit it again. The return journey was no quicker than the outward one, as besides stopping at level crossings for the guard to halt road traffic the driver also stopped at farms alongside the line, whilst the guard went to the farms to find out if they wanted the train to pick up any parcels or farm produce the next day. By the driver's side was a pile of stones, and during these stops we found they were thrown at any unfortunate rabbit or game bird that strayed too close to the train. However, during this trip they wisely kept well away. At Chichester I thanked the driver and guard for two most interesting journeys, which I have never forgotten.

WEST SU...

From MONDAY, SEPT. 11th, 1933, until further notice.   (SELSEY

DOWN.		WEEK DAYS.						
							Sat. only	Wed. only
	a.m.	a.m.	a.m.	p.m.	p.m.	p.m.	p.m.	p.m.
Victoria ....dep.	6 15	8 46	11 SO 20	—	3 20	5 B 10	7 20
London Br..... ,,	6 28	8 35	11 S O 8	1 40	3 B 16	5 B 16	—
Brighton .... ,,	7 50	10 13	12 0	2 45	5 15	6 55	9 15
Bognor........... ,,	8 30	10 SO 52	1 S O 3	3 20	5 50	7 16	9 56
Portsmouth.... ,,	8 30	10 50	1 19	2 59	5 53	7 30	9 45
Chichester .... ,,	9 15	11 30	2 10	4 10	6 30	8 30	10 30
Hunston ....arr.	9 24	11 40	2 19	4 19	6 39	8 39	10 39
Chalder .... ,,	9 29	11 46	2 24	4 24	6 44	8 44	10 44
Mill Pond Halt ,,	9 32	11 49	2 27	4 27	6 47	8 47	10 47
Sidlesham .... ,,	9 34	11 55	2 29	4 29	6 49	8 49	10 49
Ferry .... ,,	9 39	12 1	2 34	4 34	6 54	8 54	10 54
Selsey Bridge ,,	9 44	12 10	2 39	4 39	6 59	8 59	10 59
Selsey Town... ,,	9 45	12 12	2 40	4 40	7 0	9 0	11 0

Southern Railway.

WEST SUSSEX RAILWAY

SO—Saturdays only.   B-
Every effort will be made to ensure the connections with
NOTE.—The Company will not be responsible for (i) loss, damage, inconvenience or expen
servants ; or (ii) any omission or inaccuracy in
Selsey Town, Sept., 1933.   *Notice is hereby given that the Company reserve the right to cancel*

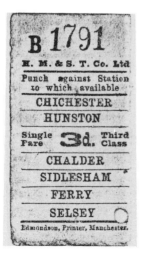

B 1791

H. M. & S. T. Co. Ltd

Punch against Station
to which available

CHICHESTER

HUNSTON

Single   **3d.**   Third
Fare   Class

CHALDER

SIDLESHAM

FERRY

SELSEY

Edmondson, Printer, Manchester.

33. Another Selsey bound locomotive gasping for water after having struggled with a former LCDR coach and a few wagons for barely two miles. Part of the platform edge still remains, hidden under blackberry bushes. (Lens of Sutton).

RAILWAY.

OFFICIAL TIME TABLE.

UP.	WEEK DAYS.					Wed. and Sat. only.
	a.m.	a.m.	p.m.	p.m.	p.m.	p.m.
Selsey Town...dep.	8 10	10 0	1 10	2 50	5 30	7 15
Selsey Bridge ,,	8 11	10 2	1 11	2 51	5 31	7 16
Ferry .... ,,	8 16	10 8	1 16	2 56	5 36	7 21
Sidlesham .... ,,	8 21	10 13	1 21	3 1	5 41	7 26
Mill Pond Halt ,,	8 23	10 15	1 23	3 3	5 43	7 28
Chalder .... ,,	8 26	10 18	1 26	3 6	5 46	7 31
Hunston .... ,,	8 31	10 27	1 31	3 11	5 51	7 36
Chichester ....arr.	8 40	10 40	1 40	3 20	6 0	7 45
Portsmouth.... ,,	9 26	1 20	2 36	4 9	6 59	8 30
Bognor........... ,,	9 30	11 11	2 27	3 50	6 S036	8 27
Brighton .... ,,	10 34	11 21	3 25	4 18	7 14	9 6
London Br..... ,,	10 55	1 31	4 14	5 42	9 B11	10 B31
Victoria .... ,,	11 13	1 17	4 15	5 33	8 B25	10 B25

NO SUNDAY SERVICES.

...uthern Railway, as shown, but the same cannot be guaranteed.
...ention of or to a passenger unless occasioned by the wilful misconduct of the Company or their
...iii) any special, indirect, or consequential damages.
...rains herein scheduled at any time without giving further Notice.   A. W. SMITH, Superintendent.

CHALDER

34. The standard corrugated iron clad building was provided here for the residents of the northern part of Sidlesham, (Sidlesham Common) the station being the closest to the parish church. It was situated on a private farm road and the company paid the land-owners £2 per annum for its use by their passengers. (Chichester District Museum).

36. Hesperus in trouble. It had only run a short distance from the station when one rail chose to lean over a little. Out came the traversing jacks which enabled the crew to lift the 17¼ ton engine and move it sideways to the line of the rails. The belligerent rail would then be knocked back under the wheels and respiked to what was left of the sleepers. There was either only one passenger or they had all disappeared on foot. One of the jacks has survived as an exhibit in the Colonel Stephens Railway Museum in Tenterden, Kent. (R. Mitchell Coll.).

35. Milk provided an important part of the income of all country railways and the Selsey line was no exception. The end was nigh as weeds spread over the track and platform and someone had borrowed the major part of the station bench. The good news was that the Ford railcar still had a complete buffer beam at the moment of photography. (Lens of Sutton).

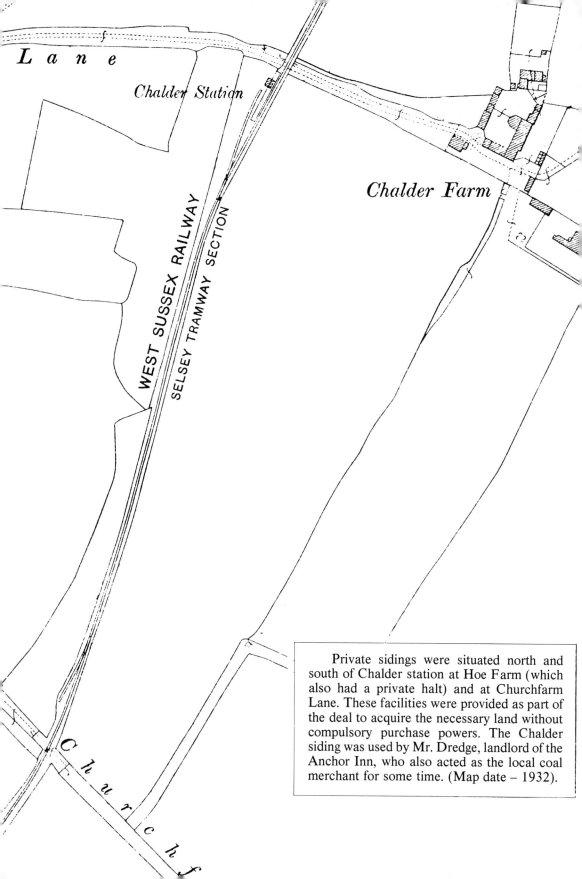

L a n e

Chalder Station

WEST SUSSEX RAILWAY

SELSEY TRAMWAY SECTION

Chalder Farm

C h u r c h f

Private sidings were situated north and south of Chalder station at Hoe Farm (which also had a private halt) and at Churchfarm Lane. These facilities were provided as part of the deal to acquire the necessary land without compulsory purchase powers. The Chalder siding was used by Mr. Dredge, landlord of the Anchor Inn, who also acted as the local coal merchant for some time. (Map date – 1932).

37. During the construction of the tramway in 1897, delay was experienced due to the slowness of the Chichester City Council in building their bridge over the canal. To facilitate the laying of the southern part of the line, the enterprising contractors decided to move their 17 ton locomotive along the public highway by towing it with a traction engine. The machine hired for this purpose was a 8 h.p. Burrell (no. 1642) named Queen of the South and built in 1892. The duo are seen here passing The Anchor, the nearest pub to Chalder station. (WSCC Library Service).

38. To reduce resistance and avoid damage to the road surface, rails were laid on their side in the road and carried forward after the passage of the engine, whose rear coupling rods had been removed. It was later named "Chichester" and ran on the line until 1913. (WSCC Library Service).

MILL POND HALT

39. A train from Chichester terminating at the halt with goods for Selsey being unloaded onto a cart ready for the horse to pull through the floods. This location was at the tail of the mill pond, nearly ½ mile from the mill. (Col. Stephens Rly. Museum, Tenterden).

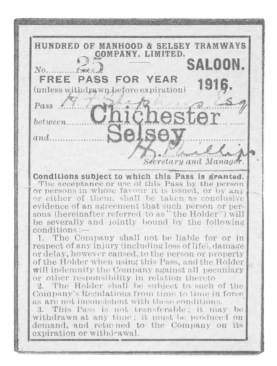

HUNDRED OF MANHOOD & SELSEY TRAMWAYS
COMPANY, LIMITED.

No. 25

SALOON.

FREE PASS FOR YEAR
(unless withdrawn before expiration)

1916.

Pass .... Esq

between............ Chichester

and............ Selsey

Secretary and Manager.

Conditions subject to which this Pass is granted.
The acceptance or use of this Pass by the person
or persons in whose favour it is issued, or by any
or either of them, shall be taken as conclusive
evidence of an agreement that such person or persons (hereinafter referred to as "the Holder") will
be severally and jointly bound by the following
conditions :—
1. The Company shall not be liable for or in
respect of any injury (including loss of life), damage
or delay, however caused, to the person or property
of the Holder when using this Pass, and the Holder
will indemnify the Company against all pecuniary
or other responsibility in relation thereto
2. The Holder shall be subject to such of the
Company's Regulations from time to time in force
as are not inconsistent with these conditions.
3. This Pass is not transferable; it may be
withdrawn at any time; it must be produced on
demand, and returned to the Company on its
expiration or withdrawal.

40. Railway emergency bus service, 1910 style. Presumably anticipating disaster, the tramway management had kept a train overnight at Chichester and was thus able to operate a shuttle service at each end of the line, linked by a horse bus between Mill Pond Halt and Ferry, which is seen here at the junction of Rookery Lane and the main road. The driver was Mr. Harry Prior and the coach was owned by Mr. John Mitchell of Selsey. (WSCC Library Service).

SIDLESHAM

41. The original station used the old spelling with a double 'd'. It was built at the south end of the village not far from the Methodist chapel on land reclaimed from the sea over 20 years earlier. (Chichester District Museum).

A 4448
H.M. & S.T. Co., Ltd.
Sidlesham
AND
Chichester
SINGLE
FARE **8d** THIRD
CLASS
HUNSTON
· AND
SELSEY
Williamson, Printer, Ashton

42. After raging for several days, a storm caused the sea to break through the sea wall during the night of 15th December 1910, flooding over 2000 acres of land in under an hour. This scene was the next day looking north at high tide. Part of the railway was reported to be under 12 feet of water. (R. Mitchell Coll.)

SIDLESHAM

HOW FAR WILL
THE WATER COME?

MOREY
PHOTO

SIDLESHAM. 2.
ATCHINC THE FLOODS

43. Local residents gaze at the inundation whilst company employees unload a wagon in the goods loop. Beyond the "Beware of the Trams" sign, a mile of good pasture land had previously been visible. (WSCC Library Service.)

DLESHAM TRAM
STATION & MILL.

45. "Sidlesham" at Sidlesham, with the company's own wagons on the loop line before the level of the main line was raised. The trolley in the foreground is of the type used illegally after the closure of the line by local lads visiting the Selsey cinema. (WSCC Library Service).

44. A battered but interesting postcard shows that after the floods the track was raised above road level by about four feet (just behind the children), the road being raised later. The land was never reclaimed again but fortunately at that time the tramway company was sufficiently prosperous to be able to afford to construct an embankment, up to ten feet high, across Pagham Harbour. During this work the station building was moved and turned at right angles to the track. It was never replaced on the platform, which was reconstructed in timber on stilts. In the background is the former tide mill which had lost its natural power source after the reclamation, but was able to continue to work with steam power, hence the large chimney. This fact has been overlooked by many local historians. The beam engine had 13 ft. diameter wheel and the boiler was 18 ft. long and 44 ins diameter. Whilst the coming of the railway would have brought cheap coal, it also brought in cheap flour from imported grains, and milling ceased in 1906. The building finally collapsed around 1920, many of the old bricks being used for house construction at Selsey. (WSCC Library Service.)

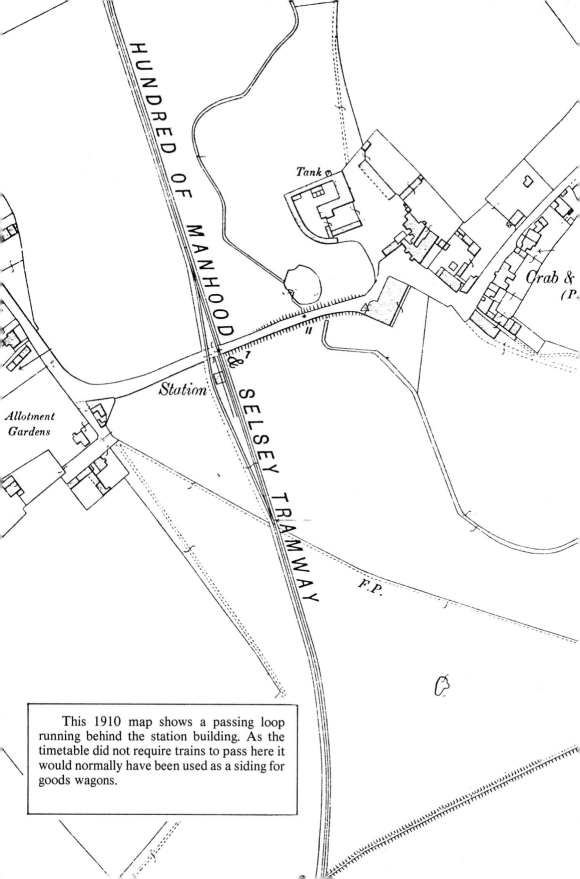

HUNDRED OF MANHOOD & SELSEY TRAMWAY

Tank

Crab &
(P.

Station

Allotment
Gardens

F.P.

This 1910 map shows a passing loop
running behind the station building. As the
timetable did not require trains to pass here it
would normally have been used as a siding for
goods wagons.

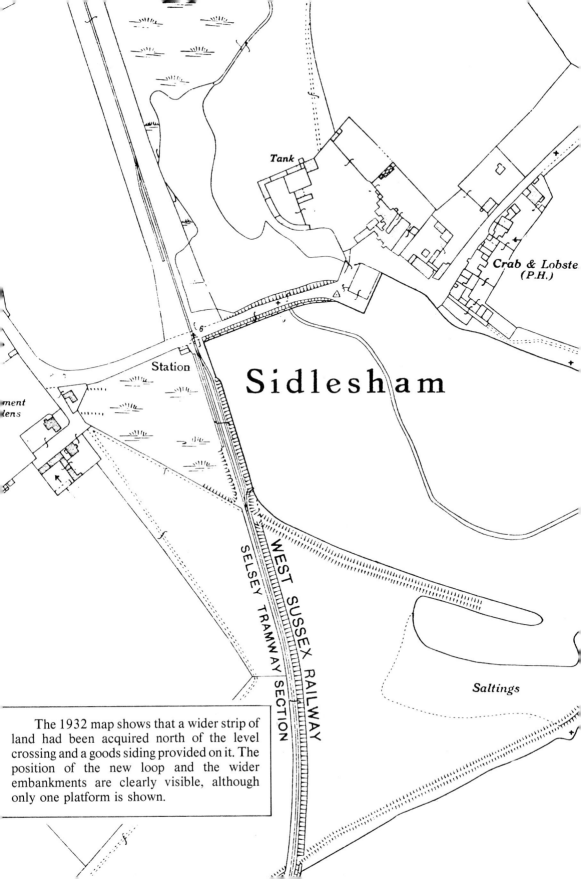

Tank

Crab & Lobste
(P.H.)

Station

Sidlesham

WEST SUSSEX RAILWAY

SELSEY TRAMWAY SECTION

Saltings

The 1932 map shows that a wider strip of land had been acquired north of the level crossing and a goods siding provided on it. The position of the new loop and the wider embankments are clearly visible, although only one platform is shown.

46. Looking north soon after the construction of the new embankment but before the erection of the platform for the loop. The solitary telephone wire provided the only means of communication along the line. (Col. Stephens Rly. Museum, Tenterden).

48. The distinctive flat topped saddle tank of "Hesperus" identifies the locomotive hauling the three Falcon cars off to Selsey. The second platform is just visible. (R. Mitchell Coll.)

47. Comment on the back of the original snapshot – "August bank holiday 1928 at Sidlesham station. The Shefflex managed heavier loads than this during the Season, and kept to time, giving no nonsense". Students of human relations will notice one girl amongst the scouts. Students of railway operation will have a rare glimpse of part of the loop line platform on the right. (Col. Stephens Rly. Museum, Tenterden).

49. The method of construction of the new platforms using former main line sleepers was more apparent after closure. The posture of the hiker reminds us that toilets were not provided on tramways! (Lens of Sutton).

51. "She would pass for 40 in the dusk with the light behind her " – so said W.S. Gilbert about the attorney's elderly, ugly daughter in "Trial by Jury." The same could be said of "Ringing Rock", at well past 40, when she hauled her mixed train across the chalk embankment in Pagham Harbour. Arnell was a Selsey coal merchant, the name still being common in the district. (V. Mitchell Coll.)

50. With only one other passenger to delay, the photographer probably did not hesitate to request a photographic stop on the shore of Pagham Harbour. Note the different levels of the rear ends of the Ford railcars. Presumably one axle had settled into a sagged rail joint. (E.C. Griffith Coll.)

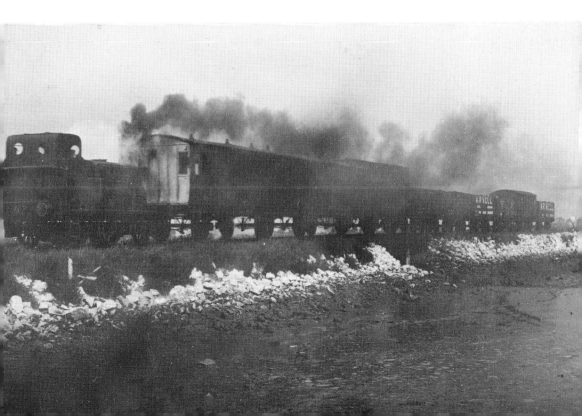

52. The simple timber baulk bridge over the channel near Ferry station standing on crumbling abutments which had been made of concrete containing marine shingle, which breaks up readily with frost. (WSCC Library Service).

FERRY

54. "Hesperus" Chichester-bound and about to cross the main road with a former Lambourn Valley coach. On the right of the picture is the support of the loading gauge for wagons leaving the siding. (Lens of Sutton).

53. The fireman is about to remount "Morous" after seeing her safely across the road on her way to Selsey. The motor cyclist has just come round the sharp bend in the road which still exists and did nothing to improve safety at this crossing. (WSCC Library Service).

HUNDRED OF MANHOOD AND
SELSEY TRAMWAYS CO., Ltd.

5210

Saloon
SINGLE
Fare

10 1D. ½

55. Looking north in 1928, the cattle grids in the track are just visible at the level crossing and in the foreground is a catch point to arrest wandering wagons. This common piece of safety equipment was not accompanied by facing point locks which would have caused a fit in the Railway Inspectorate had they known. (E.C. Griffith Coll.)

56. A collision with a lorry on 20th August 1932 turned the Shefflex railbus into a road bus in a few seconds. The crowd was evidently quite prepared to pose for a photograph. (R. Mitchell Coll.)

57. The cloth cap brigade came out on their bicycles to witness an event which was to become not unusual as road traffic began to increase. The company obtained an estimate for traffic lights but it felt unable to justify the expenditure of £39-10s. (R. Mitchell Coll.)

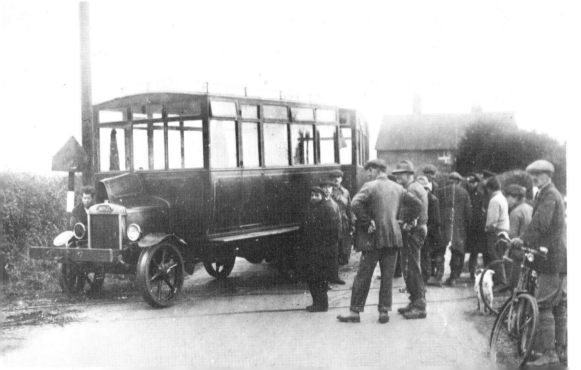

58. The main line was level at this location and so it is difficult to see why the siding was laid on an incline. This was the northward view in March 1935 with the photographer's car parked on the crossing. (H.C. Casserley).

CHEAP DAY RETURN TICKETS
BETWEEN

CHICHESTER

AND

SELSEY

(In either direction)

WILL BE ISSUED DAILY ON ALL TRAINS

RETURN FARE 1/- (THIRD CLASS)

(Children under 14 years half-fare, 6d.)

Available for return by any Train on day of issue only.

Also between
**Chichester and Sidlesham
Chichester and Chalder
Selsey and Hunston.**
Children under 14 years half fare, 4d.

Return Fare
8d.
Third Class.

1933
WEST SUSSEX RAILWAY.

Table of Single Fares.

THIRD CLASS.	Selsey Town	Selsey Bridge	Golf Links	Ferry	Sidlesham	Mill Pond Halt	Chalder	Hoe Farm Halt	Hunston
Selsey Bridge -	2								
Golf Links -	2	2							
Ferry -	3	3	3						
Sidlesham -	4	4	4	3					
Mill Pond Halt -	4	4	4	3	3				
Chalder -	6	6	6	4	3	3			
Hoe Farm Halt	6	6	6	4	3	3	3		
Hunston -	8	8	8	6	6	6	3	3	
Chichester -	8	8	8	8	8	6	6	6	3

CHILDREN UNDER 14 YEARS (HALF FARE).

Return Fares.

Chichester & Hunston, Selsey & Sidlesham 6d.

For Cheap Day Tickets see next Panel.

GOLF CLUB HALT

59. The second locomotive to be named "Chichester" (although unofficially called "Wembley" having worked in that area) approaches the halt with the 4.30 p.m. departure from Selsey on Whit Monday, 1923. The brickworks can be seen to the left of the telegraph poles and the spire of Selsey church to the right. (K. Nunn/R.C. Riley Coll./LCGB).

SELSEY T. CO. LD & L.B.& SC.R
CHEAP TICKET.
Available only on day of
issue by Trains as per Bill, and
at the Stations named hereon,
but not at Stations short of
beyond them.
BRIGHTON
3s. 8d. THIRD CL.
See conditions at back.
0034

60. (R. Mitchell Coll.)

61. (E.C. Griffith Coll.)

E.C. Griffith ably described in his book the major accident on the line in following way-

On 3rd September, 1923, the 8.15 a.m. train from Selsey, hauled by Wembley (later known as Chichester) jumped the rails near Golf Club Halt, plunged down a bank and came to rest with all three coaches derailed. The fireman, H. Barnes, was crushed against the boiler by the buffer of the first coach, which burst through the coal bunker, and killed instantly. Barnes had been with the Company for many years, and after leaving for a while had recently rejoined. The driver, C.C. Stewart, escaped with scalds. All traffic was suspended for two days.

One of the passengers was reported to have said after the accident that the first indication they had that something had gone wrong was a series of violent bumps which threw them off their seats. Had the engine not been checked from going farther down the embankment by the marshy nature of the ground all the coaches might have been dragged down.

At the inquest, conducted by the Coroner, Mr. J.W.L. Cooper, evidence was somewhat conflicting. The driver, who had had twenty-five years experience, stated that the engine was in good order and that three hundred yards from the scene of the accident he shut off steam owing to a slight decline. At the moment of derailment he was travelling at about 16 m.p.h., his usual speed, and had not received any warning that the track was in bad condition; he had complained three weeks previously about a bad joint, but understood it had been rectified. In spite of evidence by the foreman plate-layer that the track was examined daily, the general impression given was that the rails had spread and the engine dropped between them. The guard, when asked his opinion of the track, stated that "It was just as good now as when he first travelled on it twenty years ago," a statement that could be taken in more ways than one. Lieut.-Colonel Stephens, as Engineer and Chairman of Directors, was also called upon to give evidence and said that he had not personally visited this line for eighteen months as he was responsible for twelve different lines, and that the track was the original one. He supported the evidence of the platelayer and gave his opinion that some obstruction on the line had caused the derailment. After deliberation for four hours the jury returned a verdict of accidental death, but expressed the opinion that the Chief Engineer of the Company was indirectly to blame, as there was evidence of neglect in the upkeep of the track. A police constable in evidence said he could not find one completely sound sleeper at the scene of the mishap. One juryman declared that at a point within 200 yards of the accident it was possible to lift out the bolts which were supposed to hold the rails to the sleepers.

BRIDGE HALT

62. The main road to Selsey crossed the line on the bridge which was the only over bridge or road bridge of any type on the route. "Sidlesham" is seen here with a down train on the east side of the bridge in 1911. (H.L. Hopwood/Ken Nunn Coll./LCGB).

0211

S. Ty. (W. Sx. R.)
This ticket is issued subject to the Byelaws, Regulations and Conditions stated in the Company's Time Tables, Bills and Notices.

FROM

To SELSEY

VIA

3rd Class Fare . . . .

S. Ty. (W. Sx. R.)
Available on day of issue only

SELSEY To

VIA

3rd Class Fare

0211

64. Now looking north west, the Ford cars pass by, with improved engine cooling being achieved by abandoning the bonnet. (R. Mitchell Coll.)

63. Looking south west from the bridge, we see the Shefflex cars rumbling past the Trojan brickworks, with the Selsey gasworks in the distance. (Lens of Sutton).

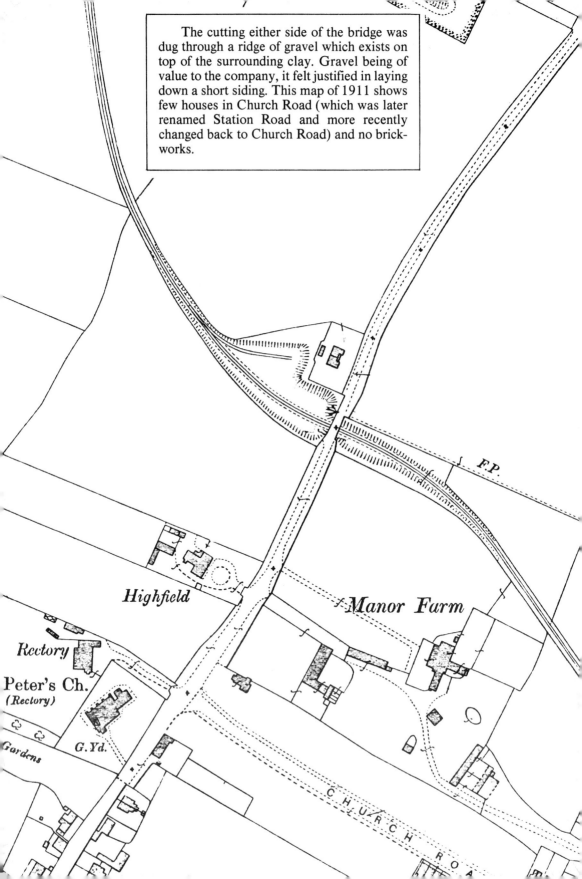

The cutting either side of the bridge was dug through a ridge of gravel which exists on top of the surrounding clay. Gravel being of value to the company, it felt justified in laying down a short siding. This map of 1911 shows few houses in Church Road (which was later renamed Station Road and more recently changed back to Church Road) and no brickworks.

F.P.

Highfield

Manor Farm

Rectory

Peter's Ch.
(Rectory)

Gardens

G. Yd.

C H U R C H   R O A

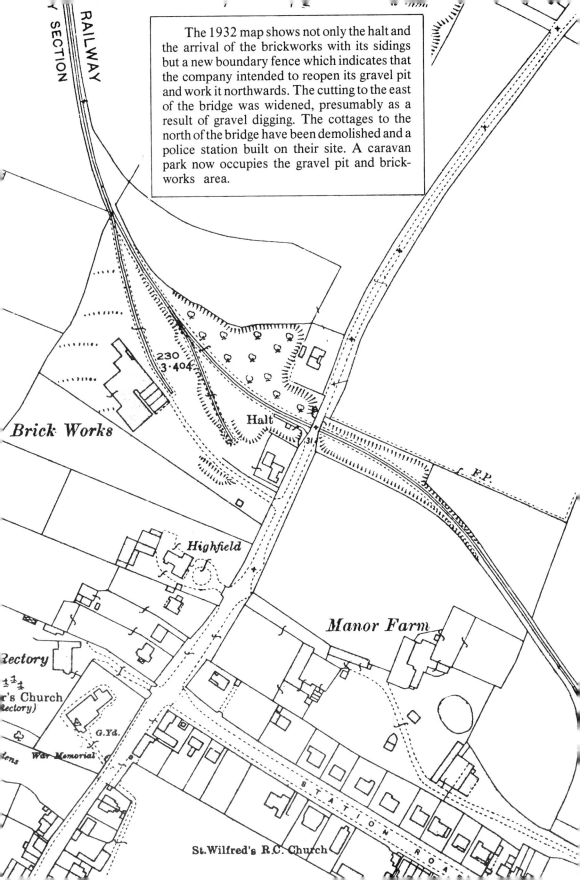

The 1932 map shows not only the halt and the arrival of the brickworks with its sidings but a new boundary fence which indicates that the company intended to reopen its gravel pit and work it northwards. The cutting to the east of the bridge was widened, presumably as a result of gravel digging. The cottages to the north of the bridge have been demolished and a police station built on their site. A caravan park now occupies the gravel pit and brick-works area.

RAILWAY

SECTION

230
3·404

Brick Works

Halt

F.P.

Highfield

Manor Farm

Rectory

's Church
(ectory)

G.Yd.

War Memorial

lens

STATION ROAD

St. Wilfred's R.C. Church

65. The interior of the Shefflex set photographed in September 1928. Pinned over the top window to the right of the door is the current year's timetable headed W.S.R. The seat backs were reversible with open centres, and in the right hand corner of the nearer car, the floor had wooden slats, unlike the Ford cars which had lino on floors. (G. Baker/Col. Stephens Rly. Museum, Tenterden).

SELSEY

HUNDRED OF MANHOOD AND SELSEY TRAMWAYS, Co., Ltd.

CLOAK ROOM.

This deposit is accepted by the Company subject to the conditions endorsed on the back of this Ticket.

Date

No. 38

ARTICLES.

Excess .... Days ....

Declared Value £ ....

Company not liable for Articles beyond £10 in value unless extra value be declared.

66. Soon after opening we see the simple standard station building, which was soon to prove inadequate, and the locomotive shed in the process of being fitted with a curved roof. The profile of a workman can be seen on the roofline, with sheeting, guttering and downpipes in the foreground. This roof did not have a long life as later photographs show a pitched roof. (Chichester District Museum).

67. "Sidlesham" at the head of a typical mixed train in Edwardian days waiting to return to Chichester. The fireman in the cab is Jack Terry, whilst guard Bill Walker is seen standing near Bert Morris, the Telegraph boy. (Lens of Sutton).

68. Crowds leave Selsey Town station to walk to the village. Controversy still exists as to the status of Selsey even today. The Midland Railway wagon is obvious; to its left is a LBSCR van, the other vehicles being HM & ST, the local line. (A. Hill Coll.)

69. The hotel was known as The Selsey Hotel until recently, when it was renamed The Stargazer, in honour of the well known local resident, Patrick Moore. The tramway station is on the extreme right of this early postcard view. (M. Cutten Coll.)

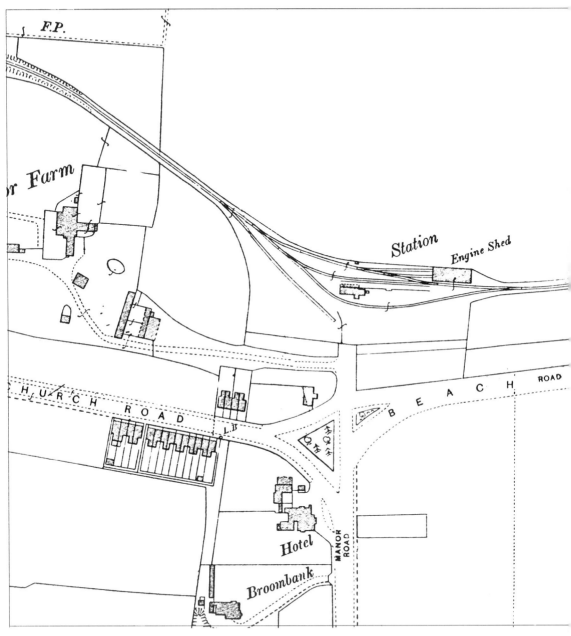

It appears that the track layout was not changed at all during the life of the line. This 1910 map shows that the goods shed had not arrived by then; few houses had been built in the area but the essential hotel had been constructed. The group of four houses nearest to the station belonged to the railway.

70. For about the first 15 years of the tramway, services were extended a further ½ mile beyond Selsey Town station to the coast, at least in the summer. Here the company's new train set is seen alongside the locomotive shed, still with its original curved roof, on the line to the Beach. The steep shingle shore on the east side of the peninsula has always been less popular with visitors than the smooth sands of the west beach. (R.C. Riley Coll.)

The 1910 edition of Ordnance Survey was the only one to show Selsey Beach station, at a time when there were no dwellings in the area. Severe coastal erosion brought the beach closer to the station site until arrested by sea defence work in the 1950's.

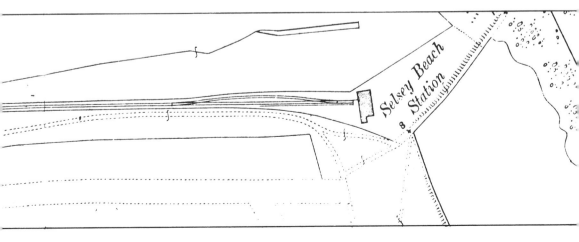

71. The base of the Beach station was photographed in 1953 with the East Beach Road houses in the background. There are reports of a tea room having been located here but there is no doubt that the fisherman had their huts nearby and were able to despatch their crabs and lobsters conveniently when trains ventured this far. The part visible formed cellars under the station. (V. Mitchell).

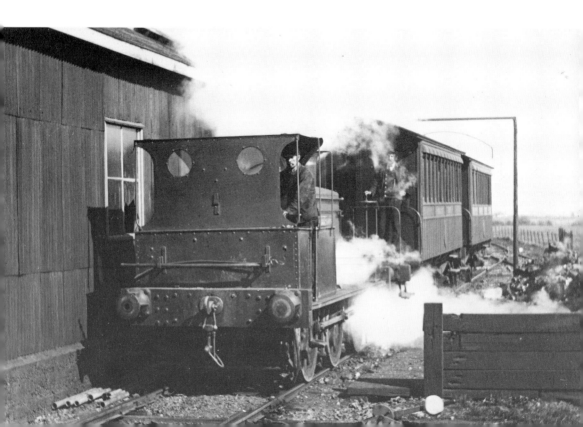

73. The gentleman leaving the rear coach of the train was E. Heron-Allen, the vice-chairman of the company and a notable local historian. He was able to announce at the AGM of the HMST on 23rd May 1917, that the little line had carried a record 105,159 passengers in the previous year. This indeed was the heyday of the tramway. Ignore the pair of driving wheels abandoned in the hedge.

The boy porter, (nearest to the lamp post) was Arthur Pennycord, who continued working here from 1917 to 1926. (Lens of Sutton.)

←——————

72. "Sidlesham" on the way back from the Beach on 15th April, 1911, with two of the three 4-wheeled coaches bought from the GWR the previous year. They had previously been worked on the Lambourn Valley Railway. The end balconies enabled the guard/conductor to move between vehicles to collect fares from passengers joining at intermediate stations and also operate the hand brake, as can be seen in this view. Note the functional loading gauge. (H.L. Hopwood/K. Nunn Coll./ LCGB).

A 5381
H M. & S.T. Co., Ltd.
CHILD HALF-FARE
SELSEY - CHICHESTER
Single Fare 6d Third Class
CHICHESTER AND CHALDER
SELSEY AND CHALDER
Bell Punch Company, Cambridge

74. A fine view of coach no. 3, built for the opening of the tramway by Falcons. It consisted of a "saloon" compartment (note the curtains), an "ordinary" compartment (note the slatted wooden seats) and a brake/luggage compartment. (Col. Stephens Rly. Museum, Tenterden).

75. Amid heaps of ash "Ringing Rock" simmers quietly whilst taking water at the rear of the locomotive shed. Its nameplate is one of the few relics to survive and is now on display at the Chichester District Museum. (M.D. England/NRM).

76. Inside the shed in 1911, the first locomotive to be called "Chichester" is recorded by a talented photographer. It was built in 1847 and was the engine we saw earlier being towed along the road. The rear driving wheels were replaced by 2 ft. diameter wheels on a radial truck which made the engine kinder to the delicate track. (H.L. Hopwood/K. Nunn/LCGB).

Bradshaw's Railway Guide was published monthly for over a century and showed the manager and engineer of every railway above its timetable. Notice that the 6.32 pm express from Chichester in April 1910 sped its weary season ticket holders back to Selsey two minutes quicker than other trains. Notice also that the 10.35 am was given ten minutes longer for the journey. No doubt this was a mixed train with goods wagons to shunt on and off at intermediate stations.

SELSEY and CHICHESTER.—Selsey.
Sec. and Man., H. C. Phillips. Eng., H. F. Stephens, Tonbridge.

Miles	Up.					Week Days.										Sundays.		
			mrn		mrn	mrn	mrn	mrn	mrn	aft	aft	aft	aft			mrn	aft	aft
	Selsey Town .....dep.	Monday only	7 0	7 40	8 30	9 18	9 50	1130	1 25	3 55	5 07	5			8 50	1 20	7 0
2	Ferry Siding.........		7 4	7 44	8 34	9 22	9 54	1135	1 29	3 9 5	5 47	9			8 54	1 24	7 4
2½	Sidlesham		7 6	7 46	8 36	9 24	9 56	1137	1 31	3 11 5	5 67	11			8 56	1 26	7 6
4	Chalder..........		7 10	7 50	8 40	9 28	10 0	1147	1 35	3 15 6	0 7	13			9 0	1 30	7 10
5½	Hunston 187.203		7 15	7 55	8 45	9 33	10 5	1157	1 40	3 20 6	5 7	20			9 5	1 35	7 15
7½	Chichester 184, arr.		7 30	8 10	9 0	9 48	1020	1212	1 55	3 35 6	20 7	35			9 20	1 50	7 30

Miles	Down.					Week Days.										Sundays.		
			mrn	mrn	mrn	mrn	mrn	aft	aft	aft	aft	aft				mrn	aft	aft
	Chichester ....dep.	Monday only	7 45	8 38	9 15	1035	1248	2 20	4 25	6 32	8 0				1120	2 0	8 15
2	Hunston		7 50	8 43	9 20	1045	1253	2 25	4 30	8 5				1125	2 5	8 20
3½	Chalder.........		7 55	8 48		1050	1258	2 30	4 35	8 10				1130	2 10	8 25
5	Sidlesham		8 0	8 53	9 35	1055	1 3	2 35	4 40	6 43	8 17			1135	2 15	8 30
5½	Ferry Siding.........		8 5	8 56		11 5	1 5	8 2	40 4	4 9	8 20			1140	2 20	8 35
7½	Selsey Town......arr.		8 15	9 8	9 45	1115	1 18	2 50	4 55	7 0	8 30			1150	2 30	8 45

77. Undoubtedly the pride of the line in its early years, "Selsey" required a new firebox by 1908 and so its boiler was sent to its maker at Bristol on a special wagon, as equipment did not exist in the shed for this work and Brighton locomotive works were considered too expensive. (Lens of Sutton).

79. The environs of Selsey locomotive shed was a paradise for those interested in unusual engines. This fine view of "Hesperus" illustrates the point. It had been built as an 0-4-0 to 3'6" gauge in 1871 for use on the East Cornwall Mineral Railway! (Lens of Sutton).

78. The bunker carried up to 1 ton of coal and the tanks held 400 gallons of water. These were amongst the features that made "Selsey" a popular steed, with the enginemen. The dented dome was of no concern to them. (M.D. England/NRM).

80. Presumably the photographer was standing on the bunker of the only locomotive in steam, hence the lack of locomotives and the profusion of coaches in this view. (Col. Stephens Rly. Museum, Tenterden).

81. "Sidlesham" over the shed pit in May 1923, with her inside cylinders unusually visible. Notice the surrounding shambles – especially the angle of the work bench! (K. Nunn Coll./LCGB).

82. "Ringing Rock" and crew on 5th October, 1925. The Colonel had transferred the nameplate from a locomotive on his Kent and East Sussex Railway which had formerly worked on the Maenclochog Railway in Wales. Maenclochog is Welsh for bellstone or ringing rock – hence the unusual name. (H.L. Hopwood/K. Nunn Coll./LCGB).

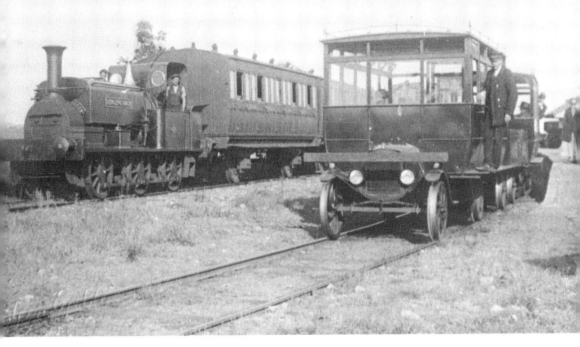

83. A posed photograph by Stephen Cribb of Southsea. This was probably an official picture ordered by the WSR soon after the delivery of the Ford set and is the only one known to us to show two trains at once. On the left is "Ringing Rock" with one of the 5-compartment 4-wheelers from the LCDR. (Co. Stephens Rly. Museum, Tenterden).

84. This 1926 view shows that a small goods shed was provided at the east end of the platform, sometime after the opening. Its presence explains why many trains were photographed at that end of the platform. Note the elegant swan neck gas lamp. International Stores were amongst a small number of firms paying for advertisement panels on the line, although here they were obscured by a seat. The locomotive shed appears to be propped up against the prevailing wind. (H.C. Casserley).

85. On 16th July 1927 this unique photograph was taken of five tramway locomotives at once. From left to right – "Selsey", "Ringing Rock", "Sidlesham", "Chichester", with "Morous" back view. The photographer persuaded the friendly engine driver to haul the three dead engines out of the shed, for his benefit and ultimately ours. (H.C. Casserley).

86. The next move was to draw "Morous" out, into the daylight to be photographed. Although fitted with vacuum brakes, they were not used and there were no continuous train brakes in later years. The cabside plate still showed "Shropshire & Montgomeryshire Railway", one of the Colonel's other lines from which he had transfered the locomotive about three years earlier. (H.C. Casserley).

87. Because of the height of the buffer beam in relation to the smokebox opening, the door had to be swung upwards instead of sideways. The fitter is about to brush out the boiler tubes which, on such a small locomotive, he could carry out comfortably from ground level. (Lens of Sutton).

88. The company had a few goods wagons of its own but most freight was carried in other companies' stock. This 4-plank wagon appears to have only one brake block but the van seems to be devoid of brakes. (Lens of Sutton).

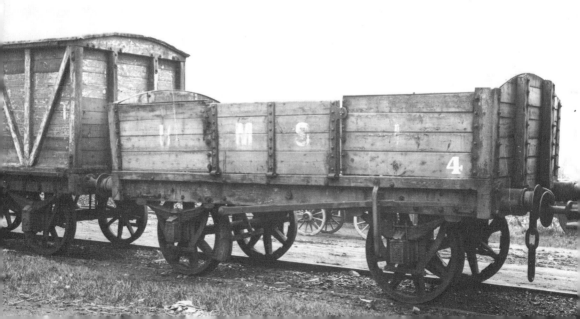

89. In November 1928 the smartly lined out Shefflex railcars were photographed outside the locomotive shed, together with the luggage truck which also had centre couplings and normally ran between the railcars. Sometimes it was borrowed by the permanent way gang as a trolley for track materials. (H.C. Casserley).

CHEAP EXCURSION TICKETS FROM SELSEY

To Places on the South Coast will be issued daily as under, from July 14th to Sept. 15th, 1912

(EXCEPT JULY 30TH AND 31ST AND AUGUST 1ST AND 2ND).

WEEK DAYS.			SUNDAYS.		FROM SELSEY to	RETURN FARES.	
Issued by Trams leaving Selsey at		Available only by Tr'ns leaving Chichester at	Issued by T'ns leaving Selsey at	Available only by T'ns leaving Chichester at		1st s. d.	3rd s. d.
Mondays.	Tu.,Wed., Thurs., Fri. & Sat.						
8.30 & 9.50 a.m. 1.15 p.m.	7.35 & 9.18 a.m. 1.15 & ||3.30 p.m.	9.36 & 10.49 a.m. 2.9 & ||4.12 p.m.	8.50 a.m.	9.51 a.m.	Brighton - - -	5 6	4 0
8.30 a.m. 1.15 p.m.	7.35 a.m. 1.15 & ||3.30 p.m.	9.36 a.m. 2.9 & ||4.12 p.m,	—	—	Shoreham-by-Sea -	4 7	3 3
8.30 a.m. 1.15 p.m.	7.35 a.m. 1.15 & ||3.30 p.m.	9.36 a.m. 2.9 & ||4.12 p.m	8.50 a.m.	9.51 a.m.	Worthing - -	3 11	2 9
8.30 a.m.	9.18 a.m.	10.3 a.m.	8.50 p.m. 1.35 p.m.	9.51 a.m. 3.5 p.m.	Arundel - - -	2 11	2 0
8.30 9.50 & 11.30 a.m. 1.15 p.m.	7.35 9.18 & 11.30 a.m. 1.15 & ||3.30 p.m.	9.36 & 10.49 a.m. 12.15 p.m. 2.9 & ||4.12 p.m.	8.50 a.m. 1.35 p.m.	9.51 a.m. 3.5 p.m.	Littlehampton -	2 10	1 11
9.30 9.50 & 11.30 a.m. 1.15 & 4.30 p.m.	7.35 9.18 & 11.30 a.m. 1.15 3.30 4.30 p.m.	9.36 & 10.49 a.m. 12.15 & 2.9 p.m. 4.12 & 5 33 p.m.	8.50 a.m. 1.35 p.m.	9.51 a.m. 3.5 p.m	Bognor - -	2 8	1 10
9.50 a.m. 1 15 p.m.	9.18 a.m. 1.15 p.m.	10.43 a.m. 2.15 p.m.	—	—	Singleton - -	2 1	1 6
9.50 a.m. 1.15 p.m.	9.18 a.m. 1.15 p.m.	10.43 a.m. 2.15 p.m.	—	—	Midhurst - -	2 11	2 1
7.0 a.m.	7.35 a.m.	8.14 a.m.	—	—	Havant - - -	2 6	1 9
7.0 a.m.	7.35 a.m.	8.53 a.m.	—	—	Hayling Island -	3 2	2 3
7.0 a.m. 9.50 a.m.	A 7.35 a.m. 9.18 a.m.	A 8.14 a.m. 10.29 a.m.	—	—	Fratton & Southsea	3 7	2 6
7.0 a.m. 9.50 a.m.	A 7.35 a.m. 9.18 a.m.	A 8.14 a.m. 10.29 a.m.	8.50 a.m. 10.35 a.m.	10.57 a.m. 11.16 a.m.	Portsmouth Town -	3 8	2 7
7.0 a.m. 9.50 a.m.	A 7.35 a.m. 9.18 a.m.	A 8.14 a.m. 10.29 a.m	8.50 a.m.	—	Portsmouth Harbour	3 10	2 7

SEE OPPOSITE PAGE FOR NOTES AND CONDITIONS.

EXCURSION TICKETS from Selsey to **L.B. & S.C.** Rly.
Stations must be taken at Selsey Station. They will
NOT be issued on the Tram.

All Tickets available for return by any ordinary Train on day of issue only.

‖ Thursdays only.

‡ 1st Class Tickets will be available by the "Saloon Compartment" of the Trams, and 3rd
Class Tickets by "Ordinary Compartment."

A—These Tickets are also issued by the 11.30 a.m., 12.20, 1.15, 2.30, and 4.30 p.m. Trams, and are available by
the Afternoon Trains—Chichester to Portsmouth—on Thursdays and Saturdays.

Children under 12 years of age half-price.

Passengers with Luggage charged Ordinary Fares. The Tickets are not transferable; are available
only at the Stations named upon them, and by the Trains mentioned, and if used at any other
Station or by any other Train, the Tickets will be forfeited and the full Ordinary Fare charged as
if the passenger had no Ticket.

On Thursdays, a LATE TRAM will leave Selsey at 8.55 p.m. and arrive at Chichester at
9.25 p.m., and will return from Chichester at 10.35 p.m. for all Stations to Selsey.

For Particulars of similar Excursions from L.B. & S.C. Rly. Stations to Selsey see L.B. & S.C.
Railway Bills and Tourist Programme.

90. The original saloon bogie coaches were left to decay either side of the station approach after they were withdrawn from service. The only sign to prospective passengers of the presence of an operational railway was a Southern Railway poster board and a wagon half full of coal. (Lens of Sutton).

91. In the busy days of the railway, the station building was extended westwards using similar materials so that the join was not visible. The battered looking Shefflex cars did not belong to the company but to Col. Stephens personally. (Lens of Sutton).

→

93. A passenger has already begun to open the door as the Shefflex set has only a few yards more to go to complete its journey. Notice that the light rail is only half the width of the wheel tread. Note also the abandoned lobster pots indicative of the merchandise frequently carried on the line. (Lens of Sutton).

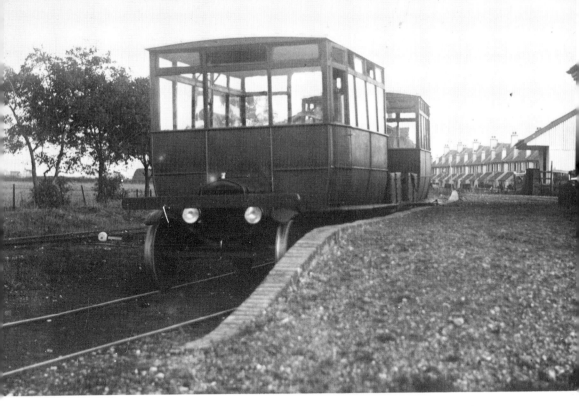

92. The white object to the left of the Ford is a weighted point lever. There were no signals and therefore no signal boxes on the line. The council houses of Beach Road have now appeared on the scene, beyond the goods shed. (Lens of Sutton).

94. "The Wreck of the Hesperus". The rear wheels were transferred from the first "Chichester" in 1914. The photograph was taken in 1931, four years after its withdrawal from service. (S.W. Baker).

95. Casually left in the shed without application of the handbrake, "Morous" nears the end of her days, still bearing the symbol of the Shropshire and Montgomeryshire Railway, but with the cabside plate missing.

The enterprising Colonel Stephens had bought her secondhand in 1910 for that line and transfered her to the West Sussex Rly. in 1924, when she was repainted. The new coat of paint gradually weathered away revealing her previous livery, to confuse passengers and railway historians! The untidy appearance of this old engine was due in part to the slanting rod to the front sand pot and the winding course of the boiler feed pipe from injector to Clack valve via the spring hanger! (C.R.L. Coles).

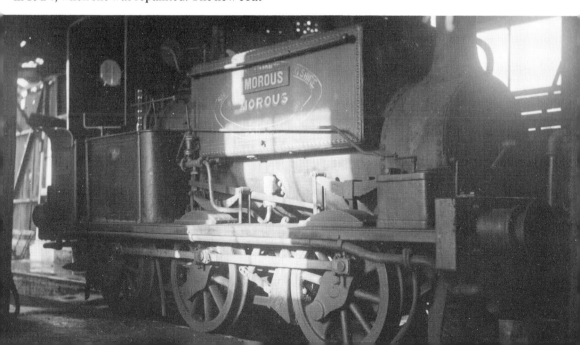

96. The initials HMST are partly visible on this cattle truck. In the absence of cattle docks on the line, animals must have been loaded at passenger platforms or with difficulty. (R.C. Riley Coll.)

14

GOODS RATES,

Station to Station (exclusive of labour).

FROM	To CHICHESTER Station.			To HUNSTON Station.			To CHALDER Station, Church Lane, & Hoe Farm.			To SIDLESHAM Station.			To FERRY Siding.			To SELSEY Station.		
	1	2	3	1	2	3	1	2	3	1	2	3	1	2	3	1	2	3
	per ton s. d.	per ton s. d.	per ton s. d.	per ton s. d.	per ton s. d.	per ton s. d.	per ton s. d.	per ton s. d.	per ton s. d.	per ton s. d.	per ton s. d.	per ton s. d.	per ton s. d.	per ton s. d.	per ton s. d.	per ton s. d.	per ton s. d.	per ton s. d.
CHICHESTER...	...	...	...	1 0	1 3	1 6	1 3	1 6	2 0	1 9	2 0	2 6	2 0	2 3	2 9	2 6	2 9	3 0
HUNSTON	1 0	1 3	1 6	...	...	...	1 0	1 3	1 6	1 3	1 6	2 0	1 6	1 9	2 3	1 9	2 0	2 6
CHALDER .... Church Lane & Hoe Farm	1 3	1 6	2 0	1 0	1 3	1 6	...	..	...	1 0	1 3	1 6	1 3	1 6	1 9	1 6	1 9	2 3
SIDLESHAM ...	1 9	2 0	2 6	1 3	1 6	2 0	1 0	1 3	1 6	...	...	...	1 0	1 3	1 6	1 3	1 6	2 0
FERRY SIDING	2 0	2 3	2 9	1 6	1 9	2 3	1 3	1 6	1 9	1 0	1 3	1 6	...	...	...	1 0	1 3	1 6
SELSEY....	2 6	2 9	3 0	1 9	2 0	2 6	1 6	1 9	2 3	1 3	1 6	2 0	1 0	1 3	1 6	...	...	...

Special Scale of Minimum Charges applicable to Consignment of Goods in Class 3, in less than 1 Ton lots. Charges are Station to Station.

RATE NOT EXCEEDING	WEIGHT NOT EXCEEDING								
	1 qr.	2 qrs.	3 qrs.	1 cwt.	2 cwt.	3 cwt.	5 cwt.	10 cwt.	15 cwt.
1s. 9d. PER TON	2d.	3d.	3d.	4d.	6d.	7d.	8d.	1s.	1s. 6d.
2s. 6d. PER TON	3d.	4d.	4d.	5d.	7d.	8d.	10d.	1s. 3d.	2s.
3s. PER TON	4d.	5d.	6d.	7d.	9d.	11d.	1s.	2s.	2s. 6d.

See Page 15 for Notes and Classification of Goods.

97. The 1922 Railway Year Book gives a total of 18 goods vehicles on the line. This 3-plank wagon mysteriously bore the number 100 when photographed in March 1935! (H.C. Casserley).

15

GOODS RATES (*continued*).

Class 1.—Applicable to consignments of Mineral Traffic, Coal, Bricks, Chalk, Cement, Lime, Ashes, Stone, Oil Cake, Corn, Manure, Roots, and other articles classified as " A," " B," or " C " traffic in the General Railway Classification of Goods by Merchandise Trains, excepting articles specially mentioned below in Class 3, in quantities of not less than four tons per truck.

Class 2.—Applicable to consignment of the description set forth under Class 1 in less quantities than four tons per truck but not less than two tons per truck.

Class 3.—Applicable to consignments in not less than 1 ton lots of Timber, Vegetables, Chaff, Hay, Straw, and all other traffic (including Class 2 Traffic in lots less than 2 tons per truck), excepting as mentioned in Regulations Nos. 13 and 14 of the General Railway Classification of Goods, which articles will be carried by special arrangement only. See special scale of minimum charges for Class 3 Traffic in less than 1 ton lots.

NOTE.—400 Common Bricks will be charged as 1 ton

10 Sacks of Wheat	,,	,,	1 ton
10 ,,	Barley	,,	,,	1 ton
15 ,,	Oats	,,	,,	1 ton

Cattle, per head 1/-.   Eight or more in one truck, 7/6 per truck.   Minimum Charge 4/- per truck.

Sheep and **Pigs**, per head -/3.   Thirty or more in one truck, 7/6 per truck.   Minimum charge 3/6 per truck.

Returned Empty Cases, Crates, &c., 2d. each.

Returned Empty Beer Casks, Kilderkins, and larger barrels, 2d. each.   Firkins and smaller barrels 1d. each.

Empty Grain Sacks or Bags (sent to be filled for conveyance by the Tramway Coy, or returned empty after conveyance) Free.

All rates are for haulage only, and do not include labour.

See Page 27 for charges for collection or delivery at Selsey.

The Selsey Tramways Company will, upon due notice being given, procure from the L.B. & S.C. Railway and place at the most suitable Station or Siding along their Line, any Trucks required for traffic in quantities of not less than one ton intended for transit over the L.B. & S.C. Rly's system; and Truck loads of goods put on at any of the L.B. & S.C. Rly. Company's Stations and consigned to Stations or Sidings on the Selsey Tramway, will be hauled from Chichester to their destination.

98. Ralph Selsby, born in the year the railway
99. arrived at Selsey, was one of several carriers operating from the station. Posing by one of his carts is Edgar Terry whilst the horse is led by Bill Mariner, who was Selsby's brickmaker at the yard that was formerly behind the present British Legion Hall. Mr. Selsby had his office in the High Street near School Lane and must have been kept busy by holiday makers before the advent of main drains. (Both loaned by R. Selsby).

100. "Ringing Rock", rather the worse for wear with its timber buffer beam cracked and an ominous patch on the smokebox. The loco shed doors were beyond patching. The Colonel hated enthusiasts and photographers – hence the "private" notice. (S.W. Baker).

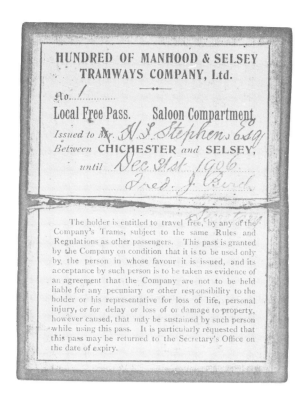

HUNDRED OF MANHOOD & SELSEY
TRAMWAYS COMPANY, Ltd.

No. 1

Local Free Pass.   Saloon Compartment.

Issued to Mr. *H.J. Stephens Esq*
Between CHICHESTER and SELSEY,
until *Dec 31st 1906*

Fred. J. Birch

The holder is entitled to travel free, by any of the Company's Trams, subject to the same Rules and Regulations as other passengers. This pass is granted by the Company on condition that it is to be used only by the person in whose favour it is issued, and its acceptance by such person is to be taken as evidence of an agreement that the Company are not to be held liable for any pecuniary or other responsibility to the holder or his representative for loss of life, personal injury, or for delay or loss of or damage to property, however caused, that may be sustained by such person while using this pass. It is particularly requested that this pass may be returned to the Secretary's Office on the date of expiry.

101. This sad view taken five months before closure shows stains on the rear end of a Ford car caused by dirty water thrown up by the rear wheels of its twin. Poor old "Morous" was safer standing over the pit than under the decaying shed roof at this stage in the decline of the line. (H.F. Wheeller).

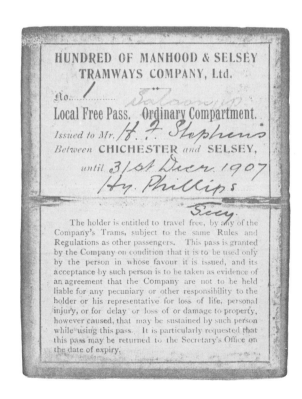

HUNDRED OF MANHOOD & SELSEY
TRAMWAYS COMPANY, Ltd.

No. 1

Local Free Pass. Ordinary Compartment.

Issued to Mr. H. F. Stephens

Between CHICHESTER and SELSEY,

until 31st Decr. 1907

Hy. Phillips

Secy.

The holder is entitled to travel free, by any of the Company's Trams, subject to the same Rules and Regulations as other passengers. This pass is granted by the Company on condition that it is to be used only by the person in whose favour it is issued, and its acceptance by such person is to be taken as evidence of an agreement that the Company are not to be held liable for any pecuniary or other responsibility to the holder or his representative for loss of life, personal injury, or for delay or loss of or damage to property, however caused, that may be sustained by such person while using this pass. It is particularly requested that this pass may be returned to the Secretary's Office on the date of expiry.

102. When the station building was extended, it was provided with a fire. The associated chimney was the only one on the system not attached to a locomotive. The shed could house six engines although only one was normally needed. (Lens of Sutton).

103. Apart from the three Falcon bogie coaches bought for the opening of the railway, the only other new passenger vehicle was this saloon car from Hurst Nelson. Purchased about 1900, it was of rather light construction and deteriorated rapidly. When photographed in 1933, it was devoid of paint with perished panels and mouldy mouldings. (T. Middlemass).

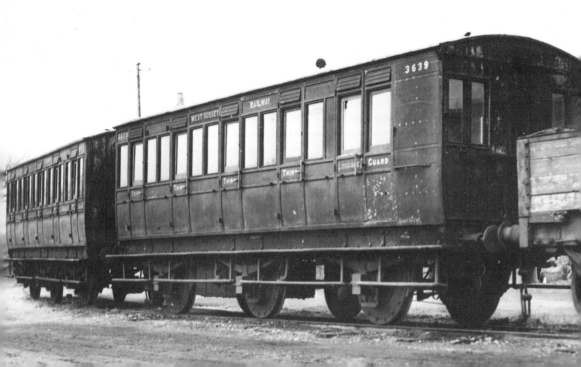

105. Many coaches only made a single journey on the line, remaining at Selsey to this day. Their bodies were removed from the frames in the goods yard and taken to the coast for conversion into holiday homes, many of which are now used permanently. This Pullman car had just lost its buffers when photographed in the last months of the tramway. It was formerly SER Folkestone car train third-class no. 205 and converted to Pullman car in 1919 and given the name "Dorothy". (WSCC Library Service).

←——————

104. With all the locomotive hauled passenger stock in an advanced state of decay by 1931, the company decided that year to purchase two secondhand 6-wheelers from the Southern Railway to use in mixed trains and on summer Saturdays, when there might be more passengers and luggage than the railcars could manage. Built for the LCDR, they were well worn when inherited by the SR. Only one panel was repainted by the WSR – the one that bore the word SOUTHERN. WEST SUSSEX was substituted, but the previous owners numbers 3639 and 1636 were retained to the end. (H.C. Casserley).

106. Services were suspended on 19th January, 1935, and a visitor on the 30th June that year found the Ford cars in poor condition and a scene of dereliction. Notice that the front wheels of both vehicles had been changed to the disc pattern following road crossing accidents. It is also interesting to note the difference in roof height of the van and the cattle truck at the rear. (Lens of Sutton).

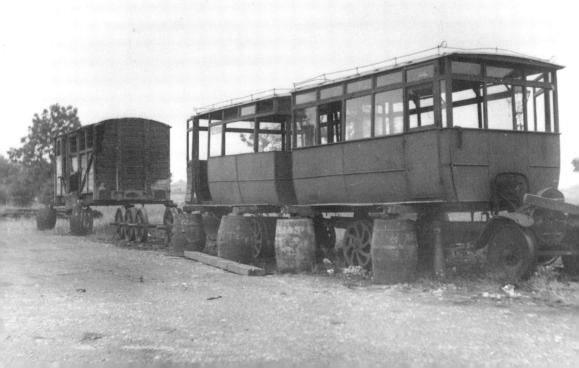

108. The washing hanging out in the back gardens of Beach Road would now remain white for ever. The vans, sheds and the weighing machine in the foreground soon disappeared, but the station remained until 1947. (S.W. Baker).

107. A year later our observer found that the van body had gone and the Ford chassis were about to be drawn out from under their bodies. Plans were made in early 1983 for a pair of replica railcars to be built on new Ford Transit chassis for operation on the Kent & East Sussex Railway, part of which has been preserved as a tourist attraction. (S.W. Baker).

109. Although this is a railway book, we feel it is worthwhile looking at the main cause of the railway's failure. Bus services started in July 1920 with five return journies a day via Hunston. From 1922, services began via Donnington and by 1923 there were 10 return trips to Selsey daily. The route number 52 was first used in 1926 and two years later the service was hourly. The bus pictured in West St., Chichester, is no. 810, a Leyland TDI with a 51-seat body built by Brush in 1929. (A. Lambert Coll.)

110. A final look at a typical scene in the line's later years. No passengers – just a little agricultural traffic – two elderly milk churns, a young calf and a tree! (Chalk Pits Museum/WSCC Library Service)